Robert Arlett
featuring recipes by Chef Carl Oshinsky

Carroll & Graf Publishers, Inc.
New York

Consulting Editor: Aris Books
Third Printing, 1992

Copyright ©1988 by The Greater New Orleans Educational Television Foundation
All rights reserved.
First Carroll & Graf edition 1988
Carroll & Graf Publishers, Inc.
260 Fifth Avenue
New York, NY 10001
Library of Congress Cataloging-in-Publication Data
Oshinsky, Carl.
The pizza gourmet.
Prepared in conjunction with the 13 part PBS
television series of the same title, featuring recipes
by chef Carl Oshinsky.
Includes index.
1. Pizza.   I. Arlett, Robert.   II. Pizza gourmet
(Motion picture)   III. Title.
TX770.P58083   1988   641.8'24   88-2907
ISBN 0-88184-377-6 (pbk.)
Printed in Canada

TABLE OF CONTENTS

INTRODUCTION

 So welcome to THE PIZZA GOURMET— though first thing to say is that this isn't just a pizza book. 'Course you'll know this already if you watched Chef Carl Oshinsky— OK, not quite an Italian, but still a well-acknowledged pizza pontiff—beaming out in living color all across America on PBS, watched him making all kinds of exotic-but-simple-enough-to-make pizzas as well as a variety of pastas and other accompaniments. For this above all is a book for entertaining, for having pizza parties— small or large, buffet or formal (though buffet style is the kind of way that Carl kindalikes to go when he caters his parties in suburban Detroit which is why, believe it or no, he makes most of his pizzas square: better control over a plush carpet or sofa; less slipping onto a tie or down a dress).

So the recipes you'll get make up a series of dishes which fit together in each chapter as a self-contained party or dinner just like each show in the TV series. But, as you like, you can swap around and change as you will and main courses can become appetizers and vice-versa in this, hey, kinda Coney Island of the oven.

So in this Introduction we'll explain some basic equipment needs, then get into basic pizza and pasta dough-making. First, though, you'll natcherly want some basic oblig. history to drop at your very own pizza parties (unless you've bought this book because your boss' spouse is having one). ■

PIZZA ORIGINS

WELL the news is that pizza history, like everything else, is bound by relativity. Some, like Ms. Mimi Sheraton, take the pizza back to Greco/Roman times, while others go to Egypt and before for flat kinds of bread which held things on top. Carl read a claim that Plato describes pizza-making in THE REPUBLIC; but Professor John Ades of Southern Illinois U. at Edwardsville Classics Dept. finds his earliest reference in Virgil.

But c'mon, nobody knows. I mean, half the world thinks that CALZONE means "pants leg" and the other half thinks it means "sock" and when you delve into pasta—well, last year the Court of Historical Review in San Francisco had a custodial battle on their hands between pro-Chinese and pro-Italian claims for the invention of the noodle. What we can say is that pizza via Italy in the Second World War, is now America's most popular food. Suzanne Hamlin of THE DAILY NEWS said that it's "the user-friendly food" of today. And Chef Carl will show you how to make a pizza far superior to what you'll get at your regular pizza joint. Even if those old fuddies at the USDA say that pizzas have got to have tomato sauce or they're not pizzas, you can get eel pizza in Japan today, or curry pizza in India. And, believe it or not, the good old American Council on Science and Health says that there's all kinds of great nutrients in pizza—even Vitamin C if you throw on some peppers (see FORBES, Feb. 13, 1984).

PIZZA STONE

So how can you in any way come close to those special pizza ovens they have in Naples with bricks right out of the lava of Vesuvius? Well children, Carl wants to tell you that perfect pizzas can be made at home when using a special kiln-fired ceramic "stone" that will soak up 20% of the dough's moisture and allow an intense (500°F.), yet indirect, heat in your oven. (Don't forget to always preheat.) Of course, Carl must remind you NEVER

HANDLE THE STONE WHEN IT'S HOT (other directions come in package on delivery). Now, you can get round stones or square stones—after all, una buona lavandaia non manqua mai pietra—but just as Carl likes his pizzas square 'cause the pieces are easier to handle at a buffet, so he finds a square stone easier to use when transferring pizza from paddle to oven— easier to find the back of the square stone which is where you must reach the paddle to. Carl likes the 14½″ by 15½″ stone for a good-size pizza; but that would be up to you.

Another great thing about the stone is that the pizza is always visible in the oven—you can see the bottom edges begin to warp, a true sign of the pizza being close to done. Don't have or want to get a stone? Carl says the product will suffer but suggests you get an oiled cookie sheet with parchment; still you'll have to keep the heat a lot lower which invites sogginess.

PIZZA PEEL

So how to get the pizza from counter to oven and back again? With a wooden paddle—properly referred to as a PEEL. Usually made of a basswood or a sugar pine. Nice and light—oil it with a little mineral oil (won't go rancid) and it will be well-seasoned.

So that the pizza will move easily from peel to stone, you need to use cornmeal as your ballbearings—make sure that it'll slide off OK. So scatter cornmeal over the peel before you put the dough on and just before you go to the oven, make sure that the pizza will move—if not, bless it with more

cornmeal under the sticking spots. Take the peel into the oven at about a 25° angle, find the back of the stone and give the peel a brief jerk back towards you so that it slides off. DON'T push the pizza forward or you'll be lost. And don't try and move a misdirected pizza when it's wet—just wait 'til a little skin has formed and then slide or fold it over as you have to. If the pizza hasn't quite got on the stone just push it with the tip of the peel. It takes a little practice, confidence and belief in the American way.

BRUSH AND GUARD

Because it's the cornmeal that causes all the smoke in the kitchen by burning up in the oven, you'll need a brush to get it off the stone after each baking. One way to eliminate excess cornmeal from falling off the stone down into the oven and causing a smokeout is to use a metal stone guard, which frames the stone along the sides and the back and helps you

CONTINUED

guide the peel to the back of the stone, etc.

PIZZA SCREEN

The stone, guard, peel and brush make up your pizza starter set (see last page); but there are other inexpensive products that you'll find helpful. Certainly you'll want to try making your first pizzas smaller until you get the hang of things.

As a training tool, to make extra-thin pizzas, and also to eliminate the need for both peel and cornmeal, you can use a pizza screen which can go right on the stone with the pizza itself stretched on top of it.

A few tips: always oil screen after washing so that the dough will not stick; don't put the dough on a screen before ready to bake the pizza; and don't cut the pizza right on the screen. Usually, when you get the dough on the screen, you can stretch it out to the edges.

EXTRAS

Now you've gone out of your way with your stone to create a nice crispy crust and if you just lay it on a counter or plate when you get it out of the oven, the steam will come right through and it'll get all soggy—so a cooling rack will allow the pizza to remain crispy until it cools a little and the cheese has set enough to cut it (a pizza cutter will help).

Carl wouldn't be caught dead in a kitchen without his big monster wooden rolling pin (even though some puristos might claim that a pin bruises the dough). Carl would only use a marble pin to keep dough cold for pastry—not for pizza or bread doughs. Some other things you might need are heat-resistant gloves for handling things around the oven, a deep-dish pizza pan and, of course, an apron to keep you from the cleaners. Might also want a 4" cookie cutter for making calzones plus a wallpaper seam roller for sealing them up—but we'll get into that in the recipes.

And if you're getting into making your own pasta dough, you'll need to buy a small, hand-worked pasta machine for rolling and cutting.

BASIC DOUGHS

Want to know a coupla things about dough, amici closa? Can't use fresh dough for a pizza in a hot oven—burn the heck out of it. Need to let it sit for 8 hours. Make it in the morning before you go to work (or at night before you go to bed if it's for a morning pizza). Stick it in a plastic garbage bag, give it a kick as you go out the door, let it rise again. And make sure that before the dough rises it gets stinky and frothy—swampy-like—to prove the yeast isn't dead. And above all, remember that the liquid (either the water for the pizza dough or the eggs for the pasta dough) is the only ingredient to be truly measured—the rest, e.g. the flour, is relative, Galilei. A reasonable list of measurements for a good quantity of dough—enough to make two good-sized pizzas or one plus a slew of calzones (about 30 ounces of dough)—would be:

BASIC PIZZA DOUGH

2	Tb. dry yeast (or an ounce packet of cake yeast)
2	cups warm water
1-2	tsp. salt
4½-5	cups high-gluten or bread flour
3	Tb. olive oil

You can make this in a food processor, in a bowl or in a well of flour right on the counter. (Of course, if you want to invest in a mill, electric even you can get, you can convert your own wheat-berries or soybeans, etc. into superfine flour.) Can make the dough maybe easiest in the processor. Water should always be warm but not much beyond 110°F. Yeast dies around 120. Don't worry too much about overyeasting—the 500°F. oven will kill off any excess.

FOOD PROCESSOR METHOD:
So add yeast to water. Pulse the machine a little, add a cup maybe of flour so that that swampy state is reached like you'd expect arrogant frogs to pop up. Add the salt and oil and gradually add flour, turning on the machine each time until the dough begins to look and sound like a tennis ball thudding against the inside of the machine. A little too wet and liquidy? Add a little more flour until it's just reasonably solid to work with.

A little oil on your hands and you can pitch it or lift it onto a floured board and then start working with it: folding it over in two away from you, turning it half a revolution clockwise, folding over, pressing, turn… fold, turn, fold. When it pushes back on you, it's ready to be stored. Into your storage bag, wait a half-hour, maybe, kick it a coupla times to let it fall, then let it rest for at least four or five hours at room temp. to rise again. If you're up in Fairbanks, put the electric blanket around it, Renfrew. The rest of a few hours will kill off excess carbohydrates and sugar. Probably should have a food scale to weigh the dough out. Cut up and store refrigerated in separate quantities until ready.

HAND METHOD:
Now you can also mix up your water and yeast first in a small bowl (knowing when the yeast is proofed by sprinkling some fresh flour onto the swamp and, if it disappears, it's OK, it's alive). Then gradually work this liquidy mix (properly called a sponge) into a well of CONTINUED

5

flour—right on your counter—working in the flour with a fork.

Or, instead of the well on the counter, you could mix your proofed yeast and flour in a larger bowl. Then mix the dough until soft and it pulls away from the sides of the bowl.

You can store the dough in a lightly oiled bowl and cover it with plastic wrap or a kitchen towel and let it rise (for a more bready dough like the muffuletta of Chapter 4, you needn't let it rise but for a coupla-three hours). For, say, the more pastry-like dough for the cornucopia of Chapter 11, add a little more flour and a little more salt to make the dough stiffer).

When you're ready to make the pizza, start kneading it again (fold, turn, fold...) and get your knuckles into it. Roll it out, stretch it out, perching it on your fists (this is the real thing, the tossing up in the air is really just for show, you'll be happy to know). So you're basically relaxing, stretching this dough, boy.

A good idea is to mark out on the floured board or counter a square the size of the peel so that you'll know how big to roll it. The high-gluten flour is easy to shape into a rough square. Transfer onto the cornmealed peel, or whatever instrument you're using by folding in half and then unfolding on the peel, or by simply lifting over with hands or on fists and shaping back on peel.

And those servings numbers they put at the end of recipes in real proper cookbooks—they're hardly relevant here, 'cause people will be roaming around the room, picking up a little bit here, a little bit there. But Carl usually gets about 8-12 slices out of his pizzas and 7-9 of his 4″ calzones from 19 ounces of pizza dough.

Now on to the pasta dough. Probably 5 AA eggs will serve you four people for dinner or eight for appetizers.

BASIC PASTA DOUGH

5	large eggs
3-4	tsp. olive oil
	Scant Tb. salt
3	cups all-purpose unbleached flour

FOOD PROCESSOR METHOD:

So let's add eggs, olive oil and salt and pulse to combine. Then gradually add—interspersed by running the machine for several seconds—your flour until the yellow tennis ball is a little more crumbly/dry, maybe, than the white tennis ball for the pizza dough. By the way, you should use unbleached, all-purpose flour for this pasta dough (though some people use semolina—use what's available and to your poisonal preference).

HAND METHOD:

Of course, you can do this without a processor: you could make the same kind of flour well that you use for pizza—beating the eggs, olive oil and salt in a circular motion with a fork and gradually working in the flour, until…

As for the pasta machine that thins the dough and cuts it, start off with quite small pieces of dough—½ pound or less (better get some scales)—until you get the hang of things and work your way up a little. Knead the dough down into reasonable flatness by using a technique of pressing, folding, turning that you used for pizza dough. Feed it through the machine at #1 setting; then fold either end inward to the middle (i.e. a fold into a third) and through the machine at increasingly high settings; until

you can see your hand through the pasta. Cut into about 12-inch sections. Let dry on paper towels for a few minutes until not quite like cardboard in consistency—but don't let it get too brittle—then either leave as for lasagne strips or pass through the cutter for whatever diam. of noodles you need. If you want to keep the noodles for later, just leave them to thoroughly dry out and then into a plastic bag and store on the counter or in the cupboard. Sorry, can't wash your pasta machine or it'll rust—just use a brush. ∎

CHAPTER ONE

Well, in case you're wondering if this so-called pizza gourmet is going to get down to it and make an old time non-gourmet pizza with that real tomato sauce, stop wondering! Because NOW Carl Oshinsky, PIZZA GOURMET, frequent-disdainer-of-sauce-on-pizza, will do it, Pruitt. In fact, just to keep the USDA in high cotton, he'll make not one sauce but two: one a classic pizza sauce, the other a more delicate sauce for a fine spaghetti dish. Then he'll try a variation of calzone that includes spinach and broccoli in a variety of cheeses. Just in case you have some of the calzone filling and some dough left over, he'll show you how to throw together a thin pizza from the overflow. And now (as that French magician used to say on the Ed Sullivan Show), let's roll the drums and get into the sauces! ∎

OLD-FASHIONED PIZZA WITH TOMATO SAUCE

SAUCE:

2	Tb. olive oil
1	Tb. crushed garlic
1	28 oz.-can of Italian plum tomatoes, crushed
½	tsp. oregano
¼	tsp. basil
¼	tsp. marjoram

SAUSAGE:

1	Tb. olive oil
1	Tb. crushed garlic
¾	lb. ground hamburger meat
¼	tsp. sweet fennel seed
¼	tsp. crushed peppers
¼	tsp. black pepper

PIZZA BUILDING:

1	lb. pizza dough
1	cup sauce
1	cup sausage
1½	cups mozzarella cheese
½	cup mushrooms, thin-sliced
¼	cup bell pepper rings, thin-sliced
¼	cup red onion, thin-sliced
½	cup pepperoni, thin-sliced
2	Tb. olive oil to brush
2	Tb. Romano cheese

NO folks. This pizza sauce just won't be as delicate as the ones you'd use for your pasta dishes. Not as sweet really 'cause we just won't take the time to remove the seeds. And, because Carl is afraid that you might find that Italian sausage making in Chapter 3 too complex (that is, too much trouble) with all that 'chinery, he'll show you a way to cheat on it in no time.

So let's get two skillets going over medium high heat, each with about a tablespoon of crushed garlic and brushed with a tablespoon of olive oil (one skillet large for the tomatoes, one frying pan for the sausage). Into the large skillet place your plum tomatoes which you've crushed and will continue to crush down into something approaching a puree.

Now for Carl's terrible secret. You know, he lives where it isn't too easy to get pork. So he'll sneak hamburger into the frying pan as the base for his sausage and forget all about the casing and the stuffing. To the burger he'll add sweet fennel seed (finocchio, they call it, out in 'Frisco) and crushed red peppers. That's it: sweet'n hot. Gotta get rid of the dead hamburger taste—so maybe some black pepper too. No salt necessary—you got cheese, you got Romano on your pizza, salty itself; so easy on salt.

Meanwhile, back with the tomatoes, Sergio…got 'em crushed down (and for goodness sake forget the paste). Add oregano and the basil (everyone, Carl wants to tell you, has a different spice threshold—go easy with your seasoning and add more if it's not up to your family's specs). So we'll add maybe a ¼ teaspoon of marjoram, too (Chef C doesn't use fresh oregano or marjoram because U.S. versions don't have your Greek or Mexican grown flavors; basil, though, is OK fresh).

You can turn the tomatoes down somewhat and turn off the hamburger pan when it's lightly browned—remember that, while you don't want raw hamburger on a pizza, it'll still cook in the oven—and drain off the fat on paper towels.

Now thin-slice your mushrooms, your green pepper circles, and your red onion, plus your pepperoni which should be cold so that it will not yield so much fat in the oven.

So you're ready to build the pizza: square on the cornmealed peel and a brush of oil. Now throw on a cup or so of the sauce and spread it around with your hands. Then a cup of your sausage on that, itself topped by a cup and a half of diced mozzarella. Then spread around your mushrooms, green pepper rings, red onion and your slices of pepperoni patterned how you wish across the pizza. We haven't sautéed any of the veggies because you want a traditional pizza—it's your choice!

So let's slip it onto the preheated stone until this monster gets golden and the bottom crust begins to warp. Then oil around the edges and sprinkle Romano on top and let it cool for 10 or 15 minutes on a rack (unless your host has trouble chewing and s/he needs it soggy. Then just lay it on the counter and let the moisture build up and seep through). ■

9

PASTA WITH FINE TOMATO SAUCE

6 oz. pasta dough
2 Tb. olive oil
2 lb. canned Italian tomatoes
4 large (8 small) garlic cloves
5 oz. butter
12 fresh basil leaves
2 tsp. Romano cheese
Salt for boiling

IF you're going to make your own pasta (and by the way, imported pasta, from Italy that is, is made from semolina rather than flour, because flour is too delicate for the trip while semolina is more *plastic*) get your old machine hooked up (and somehow—Carl can't help from asiding for the time being—don't WASH the machine or the rollers will rust—take a brush and brush it clean). Can we stop this sentence and begin again? OK: and roll it out to the thinnest number on your pasta machine. See that hand through the pasta? Well, if you're afraid to roll it all the way to the thinnest number, try maybe a "5" instead of a "7"—compromise while you're beginning. That's it, paesano. Now, cut it into no more than 12″ pieces, or how they gonna roll it on their fork? Let the pieces dry a little—but not so long that they get brittle—then run your pieces through the fine spaghetti cutter (this isn't as fine as Angel Hair, though maybe that's what you'd use if you use store pasta). If you're serving this as an appetizer, one 12″ piece of pasta cut up would do per person; if a main course, maybe 2 pieces per person. Starting out, though, don't try putting more than 6 ounces of dough through the pasta machine at a time.

Now for a finer sauce than we had with the pizza: Let's put the tomatoes in a skillet with our olive oil and garlic on medium high heat. Smoosh down the tomatoes so that the wholeness is broken down. After about five minutes remove the skillet from the heat and put the tomatoes through a mill to remove the seeds after first trying to remove as much of the garlic as possible (Carl doesn't want that bad rap of inundating everything with garlic). Then put the de-seeded (thus de-bittered) sauce over a medium heat for two minutes.

Now let's place our large pasta dish on top of a pot of salted boiling water and add the butter and about 8 broken up basil leaves. When the butter is completely melted, add the sauce to the bowl and stir gently. Remove the bowl and add the pasta to salted water (No! Don't add oil to the water—it'll just make the noodles stick). Stir the noodles gently until water is back to boiling (remember, they'll keep cooking all the way to the colander). Drain the noodles and add them to the bowl of sauce and gently mix pasta into sauce. Add remaining basil leaves and sprinkle Romano on top.

You can present this dish on an oval platter, surrounded by chopped parsley and perhaps, if served separately, in small bowls. ■

CALZONE DELIGHT

About 18 oz. pizza dough
1 28 oz.-can plum tomatoes
3 oz. mushrooms, thin-sliced
4 oz. spinach, rough-chopped
4 oz. broccoli flowers
1 cup parsley, chopped
15 oz. ricotta cheese
3 oz. mozzarella cheese, grated
¼ cup Romano cheese, grated
3 oz. fontinella cheese, grated
1 tsp. each basil & marjoram
2 tsp. oregano

BETTER have prepared quite a lot of dough—what with our old regular tomato-sauce pizza, our Calzone Delight and "Focaccia AFTERTHOUGHT." No necessary amount of dough for your calzone, but since you might want to go crazy with a large one, have a pound and a half or so ready. Preheat your stone in the middle of the oven at 435°F. for a half-hour.

Now remember the basic law of Il Calzone: make the stuffing dry. So drop your tomatoes in a colander and let them bleed dry for a half-hour by sprinkling them with salt. Then squeeze them in a kitchen towel to guarantee dryness all day long, career girl. With the mushrooms: don't soak 'em in water; just clean 'em with a damp cloth. Keep it dry. Your spinach leaves (and broccoli flowers) spin them dry with the same method that Chef Carl uses for the lettuce in Chapter 3 for the Antipasto Salad.

You can alternate the broccoli and spinach the way you do with the strawberries and peaches in the Dessert Calzone of Chapter 10; you know one on the outside of the cheeseball until used up, then the next. Or you could just combine them, both being sufficiently dry, or justuseoneortheotherit'syourchoice.

Combine the mushrooms in a large bowl with the tomatoes and add chopped parsley and ricotta. And start smooshing ladies and gentlemen. Start smooshing. Add your other cheeses: your mozzarella, your Romano, your fontinella, which is a Wisconsin version of Italian cheese (or you could use a kind of kasseri or maybe an Oregon cheddar). Mix in your spices (just remember with this Calzone mix: not too much basil or it'll get a little bitter). Now roll in your spinach or broccoli.

Now roll out your dough to about ¼″ thick on a floured surface and cut out your circles of dough with your trusty 4″ cookie cutter. Put big dollops of the mix (a good three heaping tablespoons) on each four-inch circle of dough. Then the three dry seals with clean hands—the pinch; the Mrs. Richards roller; and the braiding technique of pinch and fold (see Chapters 12 and 10). Once they're set don't bop 'em in the freezer or anything: commit yourself to bake them or they'll get all soggy.

So onto a cornmealed peel, the slits on the top and onto the stone in the wicked oven for 10 or 15 minutes. Then remove them from the stone with your peel and wipe cornmeal from stone to prevent smoking (What? You haven't even bought a stone yet, cuisinary cheapskate? Maybe kitchen parchment on top of a cookie sheet will do for the time being, but don't get cheeky). So out onto a cooling rack—which you'd better have—and sprinkle with Romano.

Serve maybe on a large dish/plate with collard or mustard green leaves as bedding (remember, stalk-end under—leaf out). ■

OUR DIVINE PIZZA OF COMPLETE SATIS-FACTION

LEFTOVERS

OK. So, you've got some of the calzone stuffing left over and maybe ¾ pound of the dough and you're penny-pinching enough to demand complete satisfactione, gringo? Well let's roll out a thin one and, since we're tired of the cornmealed smoke in the oven, let's use our training wheels, the screen, on which to lay our dough (remember, you should try not to have to clean your screen; but if you must, always oil it before using it again).

A little garlic and oil across the top (remember there's no garlic in the stuffing) and a thin layer of the traditional diced mozzarella on that. Now lay on the stuffing at your will.

How about some thin-sliced pepperoni around the edge (you must have some of that left over from the traditional pizza at the beginning of the chapter) and maybe a ring or two of green pepper and your odd broccoli top or two.

Now for a sudden trick you weren't expecting. That broccoli had stalks didn't it? Don't waste the STALKS! Peel 'em then thin-slice them and you'll have a mystery addition that tastes a little like a chestnut, nice and crunchy. Now let's fly to the oven on wings of gluttony and await the outcome for about 15 minutes. Oh yes! you were back up to 500°F.—just testing you. ■

CHAPTER TWO

So, already you are un fummagio grande, a pizza gourmet. Well think again, testa dura, for now Chef Carl will test you with some tricky dishes which would be good for a "special evening": some morel mushroom pasta and sauce; then a top of the line lamb pizza to be topped off with an Italian ice (no cream). This would be best for a small dinner party. But don't be scared—with a pasta maker, the mushroom pasta isn't so tough to make. ■

MUSHROOM PASTA WITH SAUCE

1½	oz. dried morel mushrooms
3	large eggs
3	cups unbleached all-purpose flour
1	Tb. salt
3	Tb. olive oil
½	cup Italian parsley leaves

DON'T ask anyone up in Northern Michigan where the morels are—they'll just send you 150 miles in the wrong direction. Cost about $160 a pound, do these little mushies dried. People up in those woods with full onion bags over their shoulders—or maybe nothing, not always so easy to find. Could walk all day and find nothing. That's why expensive, Tonto. But up around Glen Lake you can find morels and asparagus and Carl wants to tell you, morels and asparagus sautéed in oodles of butter are next to a rich man's heaven. So we're going to use an ounce and a half of dried morels (you could use a cèpe from Europe, as well). If you were to have fresh morels Carl hates to say it but you'd need to stick them in an oven on "warm" and dry them overnight for this recipe. So we'll grind up our dry mush-rooms for our pasta and use them, too, for a cream sauce.

You could grind up the dried mushrooms with a mortar and pestle or you could try your monster rolling pin or press down with a heavy skillet, maybe; but Carlo has acquired a little electric chop-per which makes it easier to pulverize into a fine grind—though even with the little jet you can get a stubborn dry stalk. But just discard the pieces that remain too big. Already there'll be a sweet smell.

Now let's make the pasta. Pulse eggs in a processor with a cup of flour, the salt and olive oil. Keep pulsing gradu-ally adding flour and the

ground morels until you've got a deep brown tennis ball. Out onto a floured board with more flour to knead, using the old fold, turn, fold technique (see Introduction).

So ease it through the first roll in your pasta machine, then fold twice into the center and through again at the second setting.

Now for something extra fancy, spread dry Italian parsley leaves on one half of the pasta. Fold the other half of the pasta over the leaves and send through the machine again. Now you can use one-inch cookie cutters to make some fancy designs out of our mushroom/parsley pasta. Could have a star, could have a state outline—like Louisiana State Pasta. Just roll the scraps and put them through the machine again before they're dry or save them for you and your closest—could put them into a fine minestrone soup. If you want to save any of the fancy noodles, make sure you dry them on the counter overnight before bagging.

Meanwhile, you could begin preparing the sauce for the pasta (but we'll section off the recipes for the sake of our sweet editor).

Heat the water in a large pot and salt it and add the pasta, stirring every so often. They'll puff up a bit and the edges will get a little fuzzy. Just take one out and taste the durn thing. Usually they all come to the top when they're ready and you could spoon them out but it's best to use the big glove and the old pasta insert in the pot to bring 'em out. ∎

CREAM **SAUCE**	8	oz. small fresh morels or 1 oz. dried morels reconstituted in water for 20 minutes
	3	Tb. shallots, fine-chopped
	3-4	Tb. butter
		Dash each of white pepper and grated nutmeg
	¾	cup chicken stock
	1	Tb. Italian parsley
	1	cup heavy cream
	6	Tb. Romano cheese, fresh-grated
PINE NUTS **SAUCE**	½	oz. roasted pine nuts
	8	Tb. butter
	1	tsp. marjoram

FOR the sauce, use either 8 ounces of small fresh morels or 1 ounce of dried morels which can be reconstituted in water for about twenty minutes and then squeezed dry in towels. Add the fine-chopped shallots and morels (Carl hasn't quite the heart to chop these wonderful things, but maybe they should be sliced and a couple of whole ones left for garnish) to the butter melted in a skillet over a medium-high heat. Shake the pan. Season with white pepper and grated nutmeg. Now stir in the chicken stock and add chopped Italian parsley for extra color.

Add the cream and stir, or shake the skillet, until the sauce begins to thicken and takes on a brown tone. You can pour the sauce into a large bowl and toss it with the pasta and then sprinkle some fresh-grated Romano onto individual servings. Or for an alternative sauce, maybe sauté roasted pine nuts in butter with a teaspoon of marjoram added and then pour that over the pasta. (Whatever, it's something to serve up to your boss at promotion time.) ∎

LAMB & CHEESE PIZZA

1½	lb. pizza dough
1	lb. lamb shoulder (or ground lamb)
3	garlic cloves, chopped
¼	cup sage leaves
1	Tb. coarse ground black pepper
3	eggs
4	oz. Romano cheese, grated
½	bunch Italian parsley, chopped
	Olive oil to brush
8	oz. gruyère cheese, grated or diced

SO yes, this is another top of the liner from our top of the line gourmet. Carl does his own grinding, but, of course you could stop by your finest local butcher and buy ground lamb. You can mix in the parsley and garlic when you get it home. But even though lamb is less fatty than beef, you'll want to brown it in a skillet for awhile so that too much fat doesn't soak into the dough, and anyway, Chef Carl doesn't go for putting raw meat right onto a pizza, even if it will be in a hot oven.

Actually Carl favors parboiling his lamb shoulder for about 15-20 minutes before grinding, then putting the garlic and sage leaves through the grinder with the meat. But you can put the ground fresh lamb and spices into a skillet and lightly brown.

'Course, assuming you're using your large (14″) pan to bake this monster, you should've prepared a pound and a half of dough ahead of time. The pan you'll use should preferably have a detachable bottom so that the pizza is easy to remove after baking. Just to keep things from appearing bland, let's try—if you think your stomach will take it— shaking some coarse black pepper onto the dough as you're rolling. Oil the pan lightly (it should have sides of about 1″) and place the dough in the pan bringing it up about ¾″ and trimming the edges (remember, these edges will rise up in the oven).

Now let's smoosh together our eggs (the binding agent), grated Romano, and parsley and add the ground meat once it's cooled down enough not to make the eggs immediately congeal before going in the oven. Brush the dough lightly with our old olive oil and spread the smooshed up mixture across the dough until it reaches just to the top edge of the crust and just let it rest for about 20 minutes so that the dough can keep rising.

Then into a 450°F. oven for 15 minutes. Remove and sprinkle grated or diced gruyère or swiss cheese over the top. Now place the cheese-topped pizza back in the oven until the cheese melts—just about 5 minutes. If you just set the pan on a can when you take it from the oven, it's easy to remove the bottom and pizza from the rest of the pan. So then just set it on a rack, brush the edges with oil and let it cool a little before serving this quichy kind of pizza. But "OOEE" say the litigators from the USDA. "This no can be a pizza if there ain't no tomato sauce to be seen." But "PHOOEY" says pizza gourmet Chef Carl—pizza is pizza with the regular old dough with or without the tomato, and, whatismore, si non é vero, é ben trovato. ■

ITALIAN ICE

1 lb. sugar
1 lb. water (about 1 pint)
1 lb. fruit (e.g. cantaloupe, peaches, or strawberries) Raspberry preserves and fresh raspberries as topping, plus dark chocolate for garnish.

WELL, this Italian ice may be the crème de la crème, but, know what? Italian ice, unlike your ice cream or your, uh, gelato, has no cream or eggs—just equal amounts of water, sugar, fruit and whatever you want to put on top. Start off making a syrup by dissolving sugar in water over a low heat. Then set the syrup aside to let it chill. (Now Carl is going to use cantaloupe as his fruit, but you could use peaches, strawberries—whatever is your heart's desire. Anyway, let's scoop out our pound of fruit (or whatever equal amount you're using) and puree in a food processor. Then mix syrup and fruit in a bowl (preferably stainless steel) and freeze until it becomes slushy. Take out and put in the processor for a couple of pulses to let the air back in. Then return the mixture to the freezer to firm up.

Meanwhile we can make a little topping for the individual servings—this time Carl will strain the seeds from fresh raspberries and raspberry jam and make a sweet sauce that could have amaretto or raspberry liqueur added. (By the way, those seeds that you strained from the raspberries—you could use them in a vinegar for a special taste on a salad.) So spoon or scoop the ice into individual dessert glasses, then top with the raspberry sauce and garnish with a slice of dark chocolate and dig in, for dio l'aiuta, chi l'aiuta. ■

CHAPTER THREE

Weeelll... It's Party 3-time: A great combo of pizza, salad and appetizer. Just to advise about entertainment logistics: you can make the ROASTED PEPPERS DELIGHT a day or two ahead of time—tastes better the longer it goes (within reason, that is) and it's a phenom hot OR cold (Carl has that bad habit that he can eat it anytime, anyway). And the Antipasto, too, can be prepared a day or two before your soiree—just cover it with plastic wrap and refrigerate. It lasts because of the way Chef Carl dries the lettuce, parsley et al (you'll see soon enough) before wopping it over with dressing. Then you could, like, let the sausage stuffing marinate overnight before putting it through its casing (that is, if you choose to make your own sausage). Then just make 20 oz. of whole wheat dough for the DETROIT DOUBLE DECKER PIZZA and your normal 16-19 oz. of regular dough for the GREEK-LIKE PIZZA. 4 or 5 hours to let the dough relax and you're set to tango on your cornmeal, bambino. ∎

ROASTED PEPPERS DELIGHT

2	red peppers
2	green peppers
2	red onions
¼	cup olive oil
1	Tb. minced garlic in oil, to brush
2	lb. canned (or fresh) Italian plum tomatoes
2	Tb. red wine vinegar
½-¾	cup pitted green olives

Carl likes this better than, you know, burning the skins off on a Labor Day barbecue—'cause that tends to darken them and make the peppers hard. Steam 'em and they'll be tender.

OKAY, can you jet ahead to the Focaccia of Chapter 12 or the Pita of Chapter 9? Well here's something that you can dip that flat bread into: it'll soakup this tri-color-coordinated peppers sauce. Or, of course, this is great alongside the Double-Decker coming up.

Start by roasting the red and green peppers on an oven rack with a pan of water underneath (you're really steaming the peppers) at 400°F. for 15-20 minutes. When you remove the peppers, cover them, in a pan, with some plastic wrap so that the skins will begin to blister off.

Meanwhile, chop the nice'n sweet red onions and put them in a large skillet over high heat with olive oil. Turn to medium as onions begin to become translucent.

Now heat a second, smaller skillet brushed with minced garlic and olive oil and add the tomatoes bringing them, like the onions, to medium heat.

Soak the peppers in some iced water; remove the stalks and seeds and tear them into thirds or halves. The skin should now peel off quite easily (hey, you got a stubborn little piece that won't peel off? Keep it anyway—nobody's going to notice). You can cut these peppers into thin strips of 2 to 3 inches. Stir peppers and onions together.

Make sure that the tomatoes will be sweet, not bitter, by putting them through a food mill and eliminating those seeds and any incidental skin—no need to add any sugar, just arrivederci seeds. That's it—just grind that mill away. This is not only fully nutritious with that Vitamin-C pepper, but it's good exercise, too, says Il Padrone Carlo. If you put a drop of the liquid from the canned tomatoes in the mill, too, the run will go faster. SAVE THE SEEDS AND SKIN FOR VEGETABLE STOCK IN THE FREEZER!

Now save ½ a cup of the tomato sauce for a forthcoming pizza. Place 2 cups of the sauce into the big peppers/onion skillet and stir. Add 1½ to 2 tablespoons of wine vinegar and pitted green olives. Stir and cover over a medium-high heat for 15 minutes, then let it simmer for a half-hour more. It smells beautiful, no? You can pour the sauce into a large oval dish and serve it with the Focaccia, or maybe alongside the Antipasto Salad and next to a pizza. ■

DETROIT DOUBLE DECKER

20 oz. whole wheat pizza dough
½ cup tomato sauce with fresh basil leaves
¾ cup sautéed Italian sausage
1½ oz. each of sliced green peppers, sliced fresh mushrooms and chopped red onion
Olive oil and minced garlic in oil to brush skillets and dough
8 oz. mozzarella cheese, diced
2 oz. pepperoni, sliced
2 oz. Romano cheese, grated

For a fistful of dollars, Carlo would whisper that you can preserve fresh basil, leaf by layered leaf in a closed container of salt—just rinse the salt off the leaves when you're ready to use them.

It's a cute little trick, Carl would say, to save your garlic from going rotten by pulverizing the cloves and putting them in a jar of olive oil (or oil of your choice) and getting a great flavor/oiling arrangement.

TIME now for a monster DEE-troit Double Decker that could win you friends and maybe even a promotion. You're going to prepare some of your whole wheat dough for this one—have about 20 oz. ready for the two layers, right? And that tomato sauce you stole from the Roasted Peppers Delight recipe—use it now. Warm it up with some fresh basil leaves, about ten or eleven.

Start the sauce up on a high heat until it begins to bubble, then simmer while you MAKE YOUR SAUSAGE.

That's right, Carl the Caterer does not always like to be lazy in his food prep, but he will use an electronic meat grinder with sausage-stuffing attachment if time goes by too fast. Of course, you could use a hand-grinder and then a funnel to push the sausage into the casing with your thumbs. Anyway, don't panic! Just turn to Chapter 1 and look up how Carl will make a quick-fix Italian hamburger/sausage substitute for an old-fashioned pizza. Here's what Carlo puts into his deluxe sausage:

ITALIAN SAUSAGE:
1 lb. each of cubed pork and beef (plus ½ lb. fat)
2 tsp. fennel
½ tsp. red pepper
2 tsp. black pepper
2 tsp. coriander
2 tsp. salt (if you can take it)

This, of course, will make more sausage than you'll need for even a DDD Moby Pizza, but it'll get used up quick enough when you taste it, bambino. He'll add the seasoning to the ground-up meat and use his famous smooshing technique

26

(aka knead by hand) to mix it all up. You can add about a tablespoon of minced garlic that's been preserved in oil if you like (remember? You used that oil to lubricate a skillet for the PEPPERS DELIGHT?).

Carl always sautés a little sausage before casing it—that way he'll know it tastes OK. If you're going to do a lot of sausage, you can find the casing, made from hog intestine, no less, for about three bucks—or a friendly butcher will let you have a few strips real cheap. Just rinse out the links, put them over the neck of the stuffer (or of the funnel if you're doing it with your thumbs) and feed it carefully into the casing, tying off the end. Sauté the stuffed links until brown. And slice up ¾ of a cup for your pizza (more if you're a sausage freak).

Now: in a skillet, sauté the green peppers, mushrooms and la dolce red onion in olive oil with a touch of garlic in oil added. For the pizza, Carl uses a well-seasoned 14″ steel pan with a detachable bottom which allows you to remove the whole pizza. At once. He brushes the pan with oil and sprinkles a little cornmeal on the bottom as a separator—then turns off the vegetables and covers them to steam a little—don't want to get things too oily or overdone.

Now Carl rolls out about a pound of the dough to ³⁄₁₆ths of an inch, and places it in the pan with maybe ½″ up the sides. Gives it a coat of oil and lays down 5 oz. of the diced mozzarella. You can roll out the other layer of dough (a little thinner and narrower than the first) and fold it in four until you're ready for it.

The vegetables can be spread over the mozzarella and about ¾ of a cup of sausage should be cut up and spread over that. Now the second layer of dough can go over the sausage so that we have a knobbly cover like a brim full of plums pie with a ¼ to ½-inch crust. Brush again with olive oil and coat again with mozzarella. Cover the cheese with slices of pepperoni (keep it cold before you cut it so that it won't render too much fat in the oven and make the pizza too, ugh, greasy) and cover with tomato sauce.

Last lap: slice two vents on top of the crust and place pan *on the stone* in the preheated 500°F. oven. Should take 20-25 minutes. You'll come out, sho-nuff, with a wonderful aroma and a deep red, golden-brown-yellow puffed-up beauty. Place it on a rack to cool after brushing edges with olive oil (does Carl have major stock in the Olive Oil Council of North America?) and sprinkle Romano over the top.

After cooling, remove the pie by raising the pan's bottom and eat away—but this ain't one of your cocktail hour walk-around-the-room-with-it on-a-napkin-type pizzas. Keep it on a plate with the Antipasto Salad or Roasted Peppers Delight—or you'll have a rug that'll look like Nero had been taking fencing lessons. ■

ANTIPASTO	2	heads iceberg lettuce
SALAD	1	bunch parsley
	1	large red onion, fine-chopped
	½	lb. hard salami, diced
	2	cups mozzarella cheese, diced
	3	lemons
	1	can chick peas (garbanzos), drained
		Romaine lettuce leaves for salad bed
	1	can pitted black olives
	2	tomatoes, sliced into ⅛ths
	1	jar pepper-occini
		Handful of Romano cheese, grated

DRESSING	1	qt. jar
	1	egg yolk
	½	cup red wine vinegar
	2	cups olive oil
	1	Tb. black pepper
	1	Tb. Romano cheese, grated

NOW listen! Don't let Carl catch you sneaking your cucumbers or your green peppers in an Antipasto. That's for your dinner salad, paesano. Carl (he'll take back the "Chef" for the occasion) has, you might say, developed a certain taste for this dish and that taste we're looking for combines red onions, parsley and lemon.

So you de-stalk, rough-cut and spin dry your lettuce; dry and fine-chop your parsley. Put them both in a large bowl, then add your thin-sliced onion. Add your diced salami and two cups of diced mozzarella. Add the juice of three lemons plus a can of chick peas (garbanzos).

For your dressing, put an egg yolk into a quart jar. Add vinegar, your olive oil, black pepper, your handful of

Another secret from the Chef: make sure that your ingredients are dry— gotta make the dressing stick to the salad. So Carl has a salad spinner. Don't have one? Put your rough cut lettuce in a pillow case and put your washing machine on spin—not the dryer, bambino—the washing machine.

Romano. Give it a shake—but put the top on first, Romeo—and pour it over the salad. Now smoosh away, gently smoosh: down on the outside, up into the middle. It's ready for the big parade out onto a platter, oval if you've got it, with large romaine lettuce leaves—stems inward, leaves out—as a garnish bed. Depress the center of the salad a little and place the black olives there, surrounding them with the tomatoes. Keep the presentation moving by heaping those light green occini peppers outside of the tomatoes. Now sprinkle the Romano over the salad (no salt on this one, thank you) and you're ready to serve twelve. (And listen—please don't let this out to Carl's important jet-set corporate catering clientele—this salad, covered with oil and the rest of the dressing, will last up to a week in the refrigerator if covered with plastic wrap.) ∎

CHEF CARL'S GREEK PIZZA

16-19 oz. pizza dough
Olive oil for brushing
½ cup mozzarella cheese
4 large grape leaves
¾ cup Greek kasseri goat's cheese
¼ lb. lamb sausage
3-4 fresh Roma plum tomatoes, thin-sliced
12 Calamata olives, pitted
12 snow peas (blanched in boiling water for 30 seconds)
½ lemon
Handful Romano cheese, grated

OK, a real Greek top of the line pizza. Basic white pizza dough 16 to 19 oz. been sitting four or five hours. Let's streeeetch it out, toss if you want to show off, a little, to your bella donna. Now don't make that pizza too big for your stone. The old cornmeal on the peel trick for ball-bearings. Square and ¼-inch thick on the board. A little olive oil as a moisture barrier and the diced mozzarella as bottom layer—it's good because it sticks to the dough and prevents what the fellas in the trade call "pizza slide." NOW SURPRISE, Paolo. Some large grape leaves, that's right (naughty Chef Carl likes to wait 'til maybe a corporate exec. or two aren't paying attention and he'll set out these exotic pizzas and they don't quite know what they're eating). But this is entirely and deliciously edible—didn't we say in the Intro that the Greeks may have invented pizza?

If the leaves are from a bottle, you might want to rinse them to get rid of the salt and vinegar they were packed in. So spread them all out across the pizza. Now cover the leaves with the Greek or the Hungarian or Wisconsin kasseri. And Carl likes the goat version better than the sheep—but take your pick. So big dobs of it on the grape leaves.

A little lamb sausage next to the cheese dobs. Carl makes it the same as the Italian sausage—not too heavy with the seasoning, don't want to overpower the pizza—some fresh rosemary, a little black pepper (adapt the hamburger recipe from Chapter 1 if you're in a hurry).

Now place the thin slices of Roma, plum tomatoes around the outside of the square. Sprinkle the olives over the pizza and do likewise with the snow peas. (Isn't this a contemp version of the red, white and green pizza that Rafael Esposito made for Queen Margherita 100 years ago in Napoli?)

The stone's been in the oven for an hour at 500°F., right? Make sure the pizza will slide—throw more cornmeal underneath if you need to—take it to the back of the stone at an angle of 25° and give it that little jerk back to you. If a little pizza is hanging over the stone, just poke it on with the paddle. Let it get that rich golden 15-20 minute brown and take it out, set it on a cooling rack. (Make sure that you brush the cornmeal off the stone or your kitchen's gonna get smoky on you.) Squeeze half a lemon over the pizza after you've olive-oiled the edges and sprinkle the old Romano on top. And you're ready for square pizza and red, Greek wine. Salut. ■

CHAPTER FOUR

 Dove vai? Vuoi mangiare? Then let's boogy again with Carl. This time he'll show you another dish from N'Orlins—not crawfish this time, though, but a favorite of native son Italian Louis Prima: a muffuletta sandwich with truly delicious olive dressing. Ah! Siediti, and let Chef Carl show you how. And for all you yuppies out there trying to figure out your lunch receipts for the taxman, we'll have a SUNDAY MORNING DELIGHT lox or salmon-based pizza that you could serve even before your guests are out of their leotards and leg warmers. Then a simple to make but super classy Apricots with Amaretto for afters will put you inside the dreams of your boss's wife, or husband, maybe. ■

OLIVE DRESSING

1½	cups distilled vinegar
½	cup water
2	cups cauliflower, rough-chopped
6	pearl onions
1	carrot, rough-sliced
1	stalk celery, rough-sliced
1	tsp. salt
4	cloves garlic
⅓	cup Italian parsley, chopped
1	lb. pitted green olives (preferably with pimentos)
¼	cup liquid from olives
1	cup garbanzos (chick peas)
¾	cup olive oil
1	tsp. oregano

YOU know that in New Orleans, where there are a bunch or more of fine Italian restaurants and groceries, they like that olive salad to dress up their MUFFULETTAS, baby, and they make it all different ways—a good caterer old Carl knows down there just uses green olives, celery and garlic and it's great. Course, you could probably go find your olive salad from a grocery, but Carl will give you a reasonably speedy (2 or 3 days instead of 4 or 5) way to make a salad of your own that you can pile thick on your Muff.

First, let's start a brine by bringing your vinegar (Carl would like to use wine vinegar for taste, but will use a colorless distilled type so that those cauliflower pieces don't get stained) and water to a light boil. Now pour your brine over the rough-cut cauliflower, pearl onions plus carrot and celery slices. Add salt and let the vegetables marinate under cover in your refrigerator. (TWO DAYS LATER—course, you could have saved some time by buying some pickled onions, without the hot pepper, at the supermarket; but let's be serious.) In your processor, fine-chop your garlic cloves and parsley (remember, Carl would prefer the long-leaf Italian, but you may have to use the curled). Add the marinated vegetables. Although you fine-chopped the garlic and parsley, you should now only pulse 3 to 4 times (no more than a split second at a time) the other ingredients so that you end up with varied sizes of, say, olives, carrots or cauliflower.

Now you can begin to add your green olives (black olives are, Carl feels, somewhat too pungent for this project) a cup at a time and pulse each time. Add olive liquid—like you were making a super martini— then add your chick peas and pulse once or twice more. (You don't have a processor or even a blender? Then you're going to be doing a lot of fine-chopping or crushing, Henry.) With your spatula, remove your salad from the processor and put into a large bowl. Add olive oil and oregano and you'll have enough salad to feed the lost city of Pompeii.

What with the brine and the oil and all, this salad should keep on the counter pretty well (like it does at the Central Grocery in the Vieux Carré): but if you do refrigerate, make sure that it's back to an ungooey room temperature before serving. And you're set to lather it onto the VERY NEXT DISH! ■

33

MUFFULETTA   24- oz. fresh prepared pizza
　　　　　　　　40 dough (not relaxed)
　　　　　　　　1 Tb. sesame seeds
　　　　　　　　1½ lb. sliced cold salami
　　　　　　　　1 lb. sliced ham
　　　　　　　　¾ lb. sliced provolone cheese
　　　　　　　　　Parsley to garnish

NOW your Muffuletta is the Italian New Orleans version of your Hero, Sub, Hoagie, maybe even your grinder, except it's round, maybe bigger than the standard sandwich and heavy on the olive salad that you just made. Can be served heated so that the cheese melts over the meat, but as often is eaten cold—served that way, in fact, at the Central Gro. Chef Carl is suggesting that you serve it for lunch in slices, but some of those bums down in the Big Easy will eat a whole one for their dinner.

For Carl's version, you can put together the standard pizza dough, but without letting it settle for a few hours after you've put it through the initial kneading. Use around 24-40 ounces depending on how thick you want it (Carl tends to like his a little thinner so he'll stay around 24-30 ounces). So you're kneading away, wondering if Gary Hart is safe at home for the evening, turning it clockwise, fold over, press down, turn, et cetera. Get it about 8″ in diameter and place it in a 14″ pizza pan (1½″-2″ high on the sides) that you've brushed with a table-spoon of olive earl, as they say in N.O. (By the way, to Carl's very good friend Giuliano Bugialli, a focaccia is any pizza made in a pan with oil; but for Chef Carl a focaccia is that thin pizza he's been baking with leftover dough at the end of a show.) Spread out the dough, press it out to the edges until it uniformly covers all 14″ of the pan's bottom.

So that the center won't bulge too much, put 4 holes in the middle of the dough—Carl delicately turns the sharp point of his knife to get those holes. Now cover the top of the pan with a cloth kitchen towel or with plastic wrap, and let rise 20 to 30 minutes until about double in size.

Meanwhile, preheat the oven to 375°F. with a middle rack above the stone. After sprinkling sesame seeds on the dough, put the pan in the oven for 30-35 minutes. Then set your new round bread on a rack until it's cool, baby—don't want to eat it right away, let the steam escape and get the middle all soggy do we, cuore mio?

When cool, slice the muffuletta in two—across the middle like you'd slice a bun to butter it. Now we're ready for the fun! Let's deal out your thin-sliced salami—overlapping slightly—like a friendly Vegas dealer, so that the bottom half is covered (you could use a kind of Italian sausage, or whatever is to your taste, bel bambino). Now a second layer of ham slices, or what's to your fancy, and a third layer of provolone—mozzarella if you want, but let's not get too indecisive. Now for the thick, spatula-applied layers of the salad. Pile it on, cugino, pile it on.

Press the top half of the bread on top, then cut the sandwich in half, in quarters, eighths. Serve the wedges from platters garnished with parsley. Of course, you could cut the pieces much smaller and use them as hors d'oeuvres—but then could even Marilyn von Whatever from PARADE magazine tell if that would still be a true Muffa? But siediti and eat! ■

SUNDAY MORNING DELIGHT PIZZA

1	lb. pizza dough
¾	cup ricotta cheese, room temperature
8	oz. cream cheese, room temperature
2	Tb. melted butter
12	oz. mozzarella cheese, diced
6	romaine lettuce leaves
¾	lb. smoked salmon/lox (or thin-sliced fresh salmon)
2	fresh Roma plum tomatoes (or 1 ripe regular tomato)
1	cucumber, serrated and sliced
3-4	thin slices red or white onion

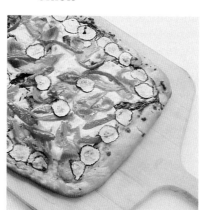

OK—this is a top of the line pizza inspired, no less, by Carl's tear-to-the-eye memories of childhood Sunday morning bagels and lox (thatsa smoked salmon belly, paesano). A pound of your dough should be ready to roll. BUT before Chef Carlo gets out his big MOTOWN rolling pin, let's mix, smoosh away, our room-temperatured ricotta and cream cheese—just using the ricotta to thin out the cream cheese, let it go a little farther in these perilous hard times.

Stretch, roll out your dough, slightly thinner in the middle, so that it'll fit on your, you got it, cornmealed peel. Since this is a brunch pizza, let's brush the dough with melted butter rather than oil as our moisture barrier.

Now the glue: the diced mozzarella. On top of the mozzarella spread out six large romaine lettuce leaves (stalk bases removed). This will provide a shield from the mozzarella on which to spread the cream cheese/ricotta mix— so put dobs of it on each leaf and spread it out a bit.

Tear the lox into 2" or 3" strips and drape around the pizza (can't find lox, John Wesley? Cut thin strips of fresh salmon—not so salty anyway). Now your thin-sliced Roma tomatoes can be spread out (can't find a fresh Roma? Get a reg'lar beefsteak tomato and scoop out some of the seeds and liquid inside).

Once Carl couldn't find any zucchini to keep up his old red, white and green color coordination. So he got the idea to use cucumber. And, behold. It was good. So run a fork down the skin of the cuke before you slice—serrate it, fancy it up. Line the outside edge of your pizza with the cucumber slices. Plus maybe one right in the center surrounded by four others. If you want, add a few thin slices of red onion to help the brilliant colors. Bless the pizza avec le cornmeal and slide onto the stone at the bottom of the preheated 500°F. oven.

A beautiful golden brown crust: bring it out, butter the edges and onto the cooling rack. Ready for some champagne and the Sunday Times on your knee and, hey, un opera de carita! ∎

APRICOTS WITH AMARETTO

4	ripe apricots
¾	cup Amaretto cookie crumbs
6	Tb. granulated sugar
½	pint whipping cream
1	Tb. butter

NOW for la crème de la crème—a sweet complement to your champagne, your muffuletta, your salmon pizza. First cut in half the ripe apricots (no need to remove the delicate skins, but remove the pits). Don't use the canned type (too watery). If you can't get fresh apricots, use a nice Santa Rosa plum or ripe peach. Now crush the Amaretto cookies (you should end with ¾ cup of crumbs).

Butter a baking dish that will hold the apricots and sprinkle 4 Tb. granulated sugar on the bottom. Place the apricot halves skin side down (pit side up) in the dish and sprinkle the cookie crumbs over and around them. Now put a rack under the broiler and get the broiler going. MAYBE a LITTLE more sugar sprinkled on top, IF you can stand it, but the cookies themselves are sweet. Five minutes under the broiler and you can spend that time whipping up your cream sweetened by the remaining 2 Tb. sugar. Then just remove the dish and serve two halves per person after heaping whipping cream on top. Just, just VAI A PRENDERLO, go get it, paesano! You're dead and gone to gourmet heaven. ■

CHAPTER FIVE

Well, well, dear hearts, you thought that last party, with its Sunday Morning Delight Pizza and those Apricots with Amaretto, insurmountable. Well, Luigi, cosi, é, se vi pare— but Maestro Carlo says, "Pensaci, Giacomino" ("Think, again, Farlee!"). For come prima, meglio di prima 'cause questa sera si recita a soggetto. Well let's drop that gig—this a cookbook not a language lesson for spies on the Adriatic. Let's get back into il teatro de la pizza and friends. We'll do two pizzas: one with three variations of pesto sauce and a kind of dessert with apple and gorgonzola and fresh rosemary rolled into the dough with Carl's pin giganti. And we'll vary our dough making for some crusty old Tuscan bread to go with some real homemade Minestrone Soup. Tuscan bread should always be given a day after baking before it's eaten, and Minestrone is always better after a day, too. So let's start with these cousins in country cooking that should be pre-party prepared. ■

TUSCAN BREAD	1½	cups water
	1	tsp. yeast
	4	cups all-purpose unbleached flour
		Pinch salt, optional

40

NOW we're going to change our dough making—using all-purpose, unbleached flour (or your own reasonable fax) rather than a bread flour—and not using oil as you do for reg'lar pizza. So let's do it the old-fashioned way—the way of Carl's good friend and fawnee, Giuliano Bugialli (Carl, in fact, bakes bread for the big G when he teaches close to the big D). Remember 'til the day of your death that Italianos don't eat their dinner bread with butter—quel insult—no, no…it's for dipping, finishing cleaning the plate, sopping up the gravy, bambino.

So let's start by making a spongy mix, adding the yeast to half a cup of water, then stirring in about a quarter cup of flour. Sprinkle just a tad of flour onto the surface and when the sprinkled flour goes under, you'll know you've had your first rising. Takes about fifteen minutes at normal room temp. Now the spongy mixture should go into the old middle of the well of flour (see Intro). Work in the well of flour as you add the remaining water (and the pinch of salt, if you opted for it) to the middle.

OK, onto a floured surface and into the old fold, turn, fold…until it comes back at you so you know you've kneaded it enough (sounds like love, huh?). Now lay the dough into the middle of a cloth kitchen towel and fold both ends and then the side flaps over it so that it's well-covered. This SECOND RISING (sounds like a Japanese Christian cult movie) will take about twenty mins normalroomtempwise.

Preheat the oven to 375°F., then unwrap the dough and flip onto our trusty old stone for about fifty minutes (under no circumstances except a fire and low insurance open the oven for at least thirty minutes or your lovely old crusty bread may fall in on you). So overcook a little so that you end up with a nice crackly that's great the next day and could be wrapped in a towel and saved a day or so be-yond. We'll show you how to serve it up with soup in just a second. ■

MINE-	2	cans (2 lb.) Italian plum
STRONE		tomatoes
	2	cloves garlic
	3	Tb. olive oil
	1	cup yellow onions, diced
	2	cups zucchini, diced
	1	cup green beans, diced
	2	cups carrots, diced
	2	cups russet potatoes, diced
	4	cups savoy cabbage, shredded and chopped
	2	cups canned or well soaked great northern beans or cannellini
	8	cups meat stock or broth
	2	oz. prosciutto
	½	cup Parmigiano-Reggiano cheese (or Parmesan), grated
	½	cup Italian parsley, fine-chopped

WELL, a lot of ingredients for this simple enough dish. Just need to get going, for tempo fugge e non retorna piu, corretto? Start off with one large stock pot and a smaller skillet going for tomatoes 'n garlic. Just heat the tomatoes etc. to warm so that you can run them through a food mill. Meanwhile dice the onion(s)— Carl even goes so far as to fine-chop them with his fancy mezzaluna—and into the medium-heating stock pot with the olive oil already heating. Now cube-chop your zucchini (Carl cuts them lengthwise in four then chops down across) and into the pot. Likewise with the green beans, the carrots, the thin-sliced and diced new red potatoes (if ya can get em) and the savoy or regular cabbage. Be sure to stir and coat your heating veggies.

Now into the same pot with half of our great northerns. The remaining beans should go through the food mill with the heated tomatoes and garlic cloves (remember, that which the mill rejects can go into a stock pot, and the liquid from the tomatoes can go through a couple of times to help the goodies through). So all the milled stuff (make sure you scrape off the pasty stuff from the bottom of the mill—that's good for the soup!) goes into the soup pot. By the way, Carl's in such a hurry that he uses jarred, pre-soaked great northerns, but you could always soak the raw ones for a day and a night or two. So those puréed beans make a nice thickening agent for the soup. Now pour in your 8 cups of meat stock/ broth (not too salty if you can help it, don't use cubes).

Fine chop the thin slices of prosciutto and into the pot with the rest. Keep going at medium heat for another half an hour (you can skim off that fatty film on top). Then down to simmer for an hour or so longer. But remember, better to refrigerate and serve the next day than right away.

OK, here's the trick: slice up the, remember?, Tuscan bread and place each slice on the bottom of a soup bowl. Then spoon your famous MINESTRONE over the bread—heart of the heartland, bambino. Let soak for a minute or two, then sprinkle a little of your Parmigiano-Reggiano over the top followed maybe for fanciness sake by some sprinklings of fine-chopped Italian parsley. ∎

THREE PESTO PIZZA

OF course, you who've taken the six-day tour through Europe know that pesto sauce usually has a basil base. But ciascuno á suo modo, as Chef Carl's frequent host Baron Nuti used to remind him. Quando si é qualcuno, a big shot of the pizza world like Carlo, you do things as you wish. So Carl will make no less than three sauces—with basil, parsley and tomato—to add color and salivating, slurping good taste to his next premiere pizza. So first the sauces:

THREE PESTO SAUCES

1	cup pine nuts (pignoli), roasted
1	cup each fresh basil leaves, fresh parsley leaves and reconstituted sun-dried tomatoes
1½	cups olive oil
⅓	cup Parmesan, pecorino, or Romano cheese, grated
2	cloves garlic (to be used with basil pesto only)

FIRST let's "roast" some pine nuts in a dry skillet over medium heat, shaking the skillet, until light brown and fragrant. Carl will use a food processor to make the sauces; but you could use a blender, a mortar and pestle, maybe even il giganti rolling pin to crush the oil out of the leaves etc. So about a cup of the chopped Italian parsley into the processor plus half a cup of oil and blend lightly. Make sure that you scrape down the sides of the bowl to get all of your precious ingredients into the sauce. Then a third of the nuts, then the grated cheese—about two tablespoons after the machine has stopped). And you've developed a thin paste.

Same thing with the basil: No need to clean out the mixing bowl, because this will be another shade of green and all tastes help each other (now where did Pirandello say that, Eric?). So let's blend in our cup of fresh basil with our oil, nuts, and grated cheese—only this time we'll add 2 cloves of garlic for variety's sake. Remember to scrape down those sides to get all the goodness.

Now for the special thing:
Better clean out the bowl 'cause it's a different color a'comin. So we'll try our cup of reconstituted sun-dried tomatoes—so sweet from the sun that they taste almost like apricots—and we develop a beautiful deep-red sauce to contrast with the greens. ∎

PIZZA

12	medium shrimp
2	oz. onions, thin-sliced
2	oz. butter
16-19	oz. pizza dough
3	versions of pesto sauce
10	oz. mozzarella cheese, diced
12	green olives, pitted
6	artichoke hearts, quartered
2	Tb. Romano cheese, grated

FIRST let's lightly boil and peel our medium shrimp—just enough to take the rawness off them—remember they'll be in the oven with the pizza. Now let's caramelize our thin-sliced onions by sautéeing them in the butter. Now let's take our piece of dough, smoosh it around with some flour, stretch it, roll it out square with moby pin and onto the old cornmealed peel. Now brush an outer ring of the basil pesto onto the dough, then parsley, then tomato—letting them overlap, making you want to move inward as you sample each sauce.

Now spread on our old glue, the mozzarella. Just inside the outer rim of the dough, ring it with the shrimp and garnish each shrimp with an olive in its center. Sprinkle on the onions, then spread the quartered artichoke hearts somewhere near the shrimp. Brush each with your choice of pesto. Check the peel's slideability then into the pre-heated oven, on the stone, at 500°F. until golden brown—your old 10-15 mins. until the bottom edges begin to warp. Brush the edges with your favorite green pesto (instead of the regular olive oil), sprinkle on the grated Romano and let cool upon a rack. ■

GORGON-ZOLA AND APPLE PIZZA

2 tsp. fresh rosemary
1 lb. pizza dough
2 Tb. melted butter
4 oz. mozzarella cheese, diced
2-3 medium apples (Granny Smith or good baking apples), thin-sliced
4 oz. gorgonzola cheese
Dash of ground cinnamon

OK, now for our not-too-sweet dessert pizza (mean, how could it be too sweet with that La Strada cheese there?), So let's try something, uh, completely different and sprinkle the leaves from a couple of fresh sprigs of rosemary as you roll out your dough (don't use dried rosemary or your guests will choke). Don't overdo it, that stuff is strong—but it'll maybe take the edge off the gorgonzola a little bit. So let's roll out the dough, onto the cornmealed peel and, because this is a dessert pizza, we'll brush it with butter

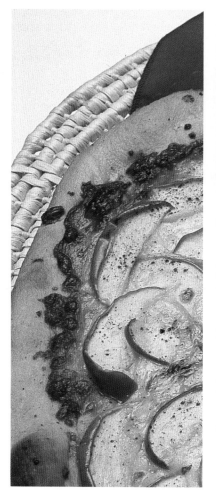

rather than olive oil or pesto sauce. Carl is using light green Granny Smiths—not, say, a mushier kind of Macintosh, but a good baking apple will be fine. He quarters, then cores and thin-slices the apples without peeling them— just removing the stray bruises if necessary.

Now a thin layer of glue, the old mozzarella, over the butter. Then an outer ring of the sliced apples and a pattern of your choice inside. Crumble the gorgonzola around this veritable art pizza (hey! Can't stand that strong cheese—

substitute what you want— come tu vuoi). Could even use pears instead of apples. Sprinkle on just a little more fresh rosemary and just a little more butter brushed on the apple slices and around the edge. Into the oven and when out a little more butter around the edge and maybe just a shake of ground cinnamon across the the top. It's delish. Carl will toast you from near or far: "Voglio per tutti il sole e la salute." Well that is if you ain't in Cleveland. ∎

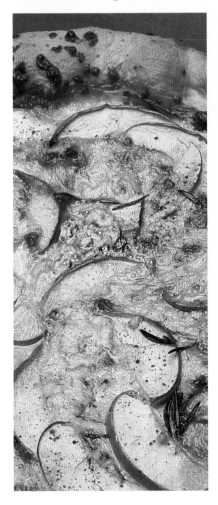

CHAPTER SIX

Still in N'Orlins Luzann, Chef Carl O. is going to prepare a special meal for his friend, colleague—and, in fact, culinary priestess to our TV pontiff—Mary Lou's thirty-fifth or so. Besides a not-so easy-to-make Streaking Green Pasta, he'll throw in a crawfish pizza—just right for that swampy, stinky, frothy mix you gotta get when you're making good pizza dough. Then for dessert we'll make a super-sweet, double-layered pan-focaccia with Thompson grapes that are coated in sugar 'n cinnamon—could Mo Siegal dream it better? The result, what with a fine tomato sauce for the pasta, will be a brilliant array of orange, pink, brown, green, yellow a-hues. ∎

CRAWFISH PIZZA		
6	oz. horseradish sauce
3	Tb. each olive oil & vinegar, combined
1	red bell pepper
1	lb. pizza dough
8	oz. ricotta cheese
4	oz. mascarpone cheese
8	oz. mozzarella cheese, diced
4-6	oz. crawfish tails, cleaned and deveined
3	oz. smoked ham, sliced
3	Tb. Romano cheese, grated

DOWN in South-Wes' Louisiana, maybe they'll boil up thousan' pound crawfishes, spice 'em up, et la bas Robichaux, spread 'em out on newspaper on tables, eat 'em up & roll it up, throw it away. Cooked that way only $1.50 a pound; but up in Michigan, Nick, whew, maybe six bucks and too salty at that. Maybe even lucky to get them frozen in supermarket. You'll want to end up with de-shelled, de-veined tails. If you start off with fresh crawfish in the shell, you'll need about 4 pounds to boil to end up with enough tails for this pizza. Can't find any crawfish? Of course, then, you could use shrimp or even crabmeat, even lobster.

An hour before you're ready to make your pizza, marinate your horseradish sauce in the olive oil and vinegar. And remember the Roasted Peppers Delight that you made in Chapter 3? Prepare a red bell pepper through the same steam-roast in the oven and remove skin by dipping in iced water, etc. Cut the pepper into long thin strips.

Roll out your pound of dough (if you want it thicker, a little more dough; thinner/New Yorky, a little less). Square off the corners to put it on the peel and stone. Cornmeal your peel and put the sucker on it.

Now separate about 4 Tb. of the slightly mellowed horse-radish sauce from the oil and vinegar and mix it up in a bowl with our old binder, the ricotta and the superfine mascarpone that we've used before for dessert. Spread this mix over the dough and spread the diced mozzarella on top of that.

Now spread the crawfish tails across the pizza and spread around IT thin slices of the smoked ham. Line the pizza—about ½-inch from the edge—with the thin strips of red pepper and sprinkle a few around the center, too. GOOD EYE APPEAL!

Make sure that this monster will move—bless it with cornmeal—then onto the stone in a 500°F. preheated oven for 12-15 minutes—until the bottom edge of the crust starts to warp and it's a sweet, golden brown. Then remove from the oven and cool on a rack and make sure that you brush the cornmeal off the stone, smokey eyes. You could cut off the edges, the excess crust so you'll have no mountain to cut through.

Brush a little oil around the edges and sprinkle Romano over the top. Cut up into about 12 pizza squares—should serve 6 with another course or two and maybe some of the Big Easy's own Dixie Beer, hey Mary Lou? ■

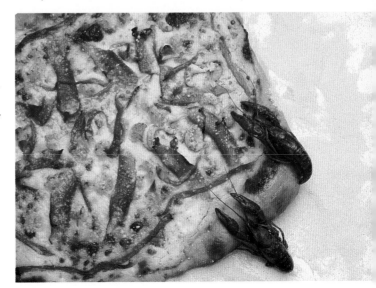

STREAKING	2	eggs
GREEN	1½-	
PASTA	2	Tb. olive oil
	2	cups all-purpose unbleached flour
		Pinch of salt, optional
		Repeat recipe for green pasta adding: 1 lb. fresh spinach
FILLING	1	lb. fresh spinach
	1	cup ricotta cheese
	4	Tb. Romano cheese, grated
		Nutmeg, salt, pepper to taste
TOMATO/	3	garlic cloves
BASIL	20	basil leaves
SAUCE	2	lb. Italian plum tomatoes
	4	Tb. butter
	2	Tb. Romano cheese, grated
		Salt & pepper, optional

OK we're going to make a species of ravioli (tough but don't panic, just take your time and tell your guests to come late)—cute little teeny pasta, streaking green pastettes, Carl would say.

First we'll cook some spinach—the pound of fresh leaves should boil and squeeze down to ¾ cup. Actually you could double the amount and arrive at the same boiled spinach you'll need for the filling. So make sure that the spinach will stay a brilliant green by salting the boiling water. Put in the spinach and cover. The spinach need only be in the pot for a minute. Then drain in a colander (you can use the drained off water for vegetable stock) and put the spinach right back into some ICED WATER to preserve that green. Now squeeze dry the spinach, first in your hands and then in a kitchen towel (if you're worried about flavor loss, Carlo will confess that he doesn't really believe that one really has spinach pasta for flavor as the eggs and flour are going to overpower it anyway—what we're into is color).

Now let's make a lateral move and prepare the filling for our pastettes. Let's take our boiled and squeeze dried and cut up spinach, then add our ricotta, Romano, nutmeg, salt and pepper and mix it all together. You'll want to transfer this into a pastry bag so that you can pipe it onto the pasta squares. If you wanted to prepare this ahead of time you could keep it in the refrigerator.

Now, back to the pasta making. Let's start with the yellow (can't make yellow from green, but can do reverse): Mix in your food processor 2 eggs, your olive oil and maybe ½ cup of flour. Blend slowly. Blend in more flour until the dough is almost dry and crumbly. Same procedure for the green pasta except that you'll add your spinach—which will make it a little wetter. Gradually add in the flour, blending until you see and hear that tennis ball effect. With both yellow and green pasta now removed from the machine, turn and knead them just as you would your regular pizza or pasta doughs. If it's all still a little too wet, you can always knead in more flour. It should be kind of tight so that when you push it in it'll push back at you.

OK—time to hook up the rolling machine. You want the dough to be a little wet, now—not too much flour—because we want the two pastas to stick together soon. Roll out the green at setting 2, so that it gets to about ⅛ of an inch thick. Repeat with the yellow pasta. Now square off the two reams of pasta and cut them lengthwise with a pasta cutter into ⅜-inch strips, perhaps in 8-inch lengths. Now arrange the strips into sets of alternating candy-stripes: yellow, green, yellow, green, yellow. If needed, moisten the edges of the strips so that they stick together.

VERY CAREFULLY put the combined strips through the machine for a couple of settings until they're at ¹⁄₁₆ of an inch thick. Now cut the pasta across in 3″ pieces. So that you have a series of 3″ by 4″ pieces. The toughest part is over! Now pipe (or if you've no pastry bag, carefully spoon) the filling onto the pasta pieces—about a tablespoon's worth onto each pastette—across the stripes. Now roll up the pastettes, like a cigarette, and twist the ends like a Christmas Cracker. You end up with a green & yellow version of an unwrapped tootsie roll. You could now transfer your rolls onto a lightly floured, shallow dish and refrigerate them while you're preparing a light tomato sauce.

In a high-heated skillet add the garlic and half of the fresh basil leaves to your canned plum tomatoes and smoosh them down. Now press the tomatoes through a strainer or through a food mill so that you get rid of seeds and skin and end up with a very fine sauce sans most garlic and basil but with their flavor.

In a pan melt the butter and add the strained tomatoes and put on low heat to reduce slightly.

Into boiling, salted water (no oil for pasta, remember) with an INSERT in the boiler so that you can easily remove the little rolls (an insert is an equivalent to that thing they put french fries in and plunge in and out of the fat), place your pastettes. Boil for 3 or 4 minutes. Then remove the insert, let them drain off a little and place them in a shallow dish.

Spoon the sauce onto oval plates and place the rolls in them (three for an appetizer, maybe six for dinner per person). Then garnish with remaining basil leaves and sprinkle a little Romano over the dish. So fine, paesano, Italian colors and all! ∎

FOCACCIA	¾	cup sugar
WITH FRESH	4	cups (about 2 lb.) seedless,
GRAPES		red grapes
	1	tsp. cinnamon
	1½	lb. pizza dough
	2	Tb. melted butter

REMEMBER that Carl says that focaccia has all kinds of murky definitions. Well, this one is gonna be in a pan—a two-decker dessert pizza, no less. We'll be using a well-buttered 14″ pan with 1½″ sides and a detachable bottom. First let's pour all but 2 teaspoons of the sugar over the grapes in a bowl. Maybe add a little cinnamon. Roll the grapes around so that they're well-coated (sometimes Carl will just eat grapes that have been dipped in egg-white and then sugar—delicious).

Now let's roll out our pound piece of dough so that it can be placed into the buttered

(and just slightly cornmealed) pan so that it hangs over the edges. Brush the bottom of the dough with butter. Now spread all but ¾ of a cup of the sugared grapes around the dough. Now roll out the smaller piece of dough and place it on top of the grapes, but without going beyond the pan's edge.

Place the remaining grapes around the outside of the second layer of dough and fold the overhanging edge of the bottom layer of dough over them. Thus nobody will end up with just a plain piece of outside dough. Now vent the top layer an inch or so down the middle, brush with butter and sprinkle the remaining sugar with a little cinnamon over the top—you get a kind of brown sugar effect. Then right onto the stone at about 400°F. for 15-20 minutes. Remove. Give it another brush of butter. Let cool. This could become a luxury item if served with, maybe, mascarpone thinned down with a little whipping cream and streaked with honey, vanilla. Ah, again Carl, you have reached perfection. ■

CHAPTER SEVEN

 Well maybe that Streaking Green Pasta was the most delicate of dishes in this WHOLE DURN BOOK; certainly, it was the most difficult to make, no Umberto? Here, though, are a cluster of delicate dishes not so difficult to make. First, since Carlo made Italian Sausage before, he'll show you now how-a to-a do-a great seafood sausage with fresh salmon and shrimp or variation. Then a variation on pizza dough using potatoes for natural yeast as base for a vegetable pizza. Then giant tortellis with Italian mushroom dressing and a quick—honeysuckle, we're talking a minute or less— but delicious dessert with a special cream over raspberries. Forget the hot tuna to-nite, Jorma, don't hesitate to jump right in now with our salmon mousse sausage with tomato sauce. ∎

SEAFOOD SAUSAGE

1 medium carrot, peeled and sliced
10 oz. fresh spinach
Salt for boiling
2 lb. peeled and deveined shrimp (crawfish or lobster can be substituted)
½-¾ lb. skinned and boned fresh salmon, well-chilled
½ cup whipping cream, well-chilled
1 egg
⅛ tsp. each white pepper & nutmeg
Italian parsley, for garnish

FOR starters, let's remember that you need to end up with your salmon sans skin and bone and your shrimps beheaded, without shells and deveined. So what might start out as 2 pounds of shrimp will end up about a pound. Likewise, the salmon would start as a pound piece and end up half to three-quarters of a pound. Course, you could buy them both already prepared as you need them.

First let's get our large pot of water (salted to preserve coloration) boiling. Slice the peeled carrot down the center and then chop in half and place in boiling water (it's best to use a pasta insert as you did if you made the Streaking Green Pasta in CHAPTER 6). After a minute or so add the fresh spinach into the same boiling water. Boil for about two minutes then remove spinach and carrot and place in iced water—so that you, again, preserve coloration and can handle them quickly. HINT-HINT: you can use the water that you boiled the spinach and carrot in as a stock base. Meanwhile, put the shrimp in a pan of tepid water and bring them to a boil—Carl doesn't see any need to season them now: don't want to overwhelm the final product.

Squeeze dry the spinach just as you did when making the spinach pasta and also remove the carrot from the iced water. Then spoon out the shrimp (only about 3 minutes cooking time needed) and let them cool, also, in the iced water—so that you retard cooking and can also quickly handle them without refrigerating.

Now fine chop the dried-out spinach. (Carl uses a mezza-luna—a curved-bladed knife with handles at both ends—truly Italian, invented at the request of Caligula.) Then thin-slice and fine-chop the carrot. The shrimp, too, should be fine-chopped. These three ingredients won't go into the food processor along with the salmon, etc., because Carl wants you actually to experience their taste; so fine, fine pieces, please.

The salmon, you'd hope to get skinned and filleted, but should you need to skin and bone it yourself, start with the tail, where the bone is, then skin along the bottom. You can separate meat from remaining bone with a spoon. Don't worry about preserving texture, 'cause it's all goin' in the processor or blender anyway to form a mousse.

So into the processor—use your S-blade—with the salmon (yes, you could try the blender, but it'll be somewhat arduous getting everything moussed down). Then add the half cup of well-chilled cream, plus a fresh egg—these are thickening agents, Romeo. Now your dash of white pepper and fresh-grated nutmeg (Carl does like that fresh Italianate nutmeg) and let it whirr, baby, whirrrr. Start to thicken up and that whirr will become a murmur. Now you can mix your fine-chopped carrot, spinach and shrimp into the mousse and you're ready for stuffing the sausage.

Stuff just as you did with the Italian sausage in CHAPTER THREE—either using the fancy sausage maker or just a simple old funnel and plunger if your thumbs are too dainty. Remember to tie off one end and then the other when stuffing is completed so that you end up with about a twenty-four to thirty-inch length of sausage which can be twisted into maybe four-inch links if you want.

You can poke the links a little with a sharp knife tip so that they won't explode on you. Now heat up the water you boiled the shrimp in (or you could use vegetable or fish stock) and poach (as opposed to rapidly boiling) the links for about eight minutes.

Now, while the sausage cools—it actually might best be served chilled a little—prepare that same fine tomato/garlic/basil sauce that accompanied the Streaking Green Pasta tootsie rolls in CHAPTER 6 (of course, you could use your favorite cream, mushroom or whatever alternative sauce you desire). Spoon the sauce onto individual dishes (oval if ya got it) and arrange maybe six ¼- or ⅕-inch slices of the sausage on one half of the sauce-laden dish with, hey, Italian parsley on the other half. Maybe serve with a Tuscan bread (which Chef Carl showed you how to make in CHAPTER 5) a basic focaccia or even the, hey, potato-dough based pizza which is a-comin' right up! ∎

POTATO DOUGH VEGETABLE PIZZA

DOUGH:
2   medium potatoes, peeled
3   cups water
1   tsp. dry yeast
3   cups high-gluten (bread) flour
¼   cup olive oil
2   tsp. salt

PIZZA BUILDING:
1   cup broccoli tops
12 asparagus tips
    Oil for cooking
10 oz. mozzarella cheese, grated
1   red bell pepper, sliced in rings
3   oz. gruyère or swiss cheese
    Olive oil to brush
    Grated Romano cheese, for garnish

SO want to go natural and airy and breezy? A bubblier kind of pizza made the old-fashioned way (just jet over to the old country and you'll see it'sa true). Here's that ch-ch-chameleon Carl showin' you a different way again: First let's peel our potatoes (one large, two medium, or three small of whatever kind you've got), boil 'em up in two cups of water (and don't throw that water away, wastrel). Then cut 'em in ¼s or ⅛s and put 'em through a food mill, into a large pan, and mash with a fork or whatever to get rid of those nasty lumps, Luigi. Now add about 1½ cups of the water from the potato boil. Keep stirring and mashing and stir in the yeast as leavening insurance—add a little flour, let it get extra soggy, swampy and all that bubblefoamjazz of, hey, the activation process. Now add maybe ½ cup more water as you stir and then a whole cup of flour, pinch or so of salt; then the oil.

Work it around, now, add maybe a cup more flour, some more water as you move toward that old pizza dough feeling, maybe changing to a rubber spatula as you mix and stir. Sooner or later, though, Carl will just have to get those mitts in there, get TACTILE, adding his flour as needed (get that pun?) and the dough gets firmer and drier (though you might knead a little water to pick up some of the stray pieces).

Now pitch the dough out onto a floured board or counter and start the old kneading process proper—fold in, turn halfway, fold, turn… Then oil the pan you were using, put the dough back, cover with plastic wrap and let your dough rise at least for a few hours and refrigerate. Then roll it out, stretch it out with yer fists, roll it out and get it all ready for your peel.

Meanwhile, sauté your broccoli tops and asparagus tips in an oiled skillet for just a minute, then cover and let sit for five minutes. Oil your dough on the cornmealed peel, then spread the old mozzarella glue across. Now spread the broccoli and asparagus, plus red pepper rings, across to obtain the old tricolor effect. Sprinkle the grated gruyère/swiss or whatever you've chosen for the top. Then onto the preheated stone at 500°F. for 10-15 minutes— until the old bottom edges warp, right?

Then brush with olive oil around edges, a little Romano over the top. Onto the cooling rack. Then cut square with your giant pizza knife. ∎

THE BIG TORTELLI (or A Tortelli to Remember)

2 oz. reconstituted sun-dried tomatoes
1½- oz. dried porcini
2 mushrooms (shiitake could be substituted)
About 1 lb. basic pasta dough
8 oz. ricotta cheese
½ cup grated Romano cheese
2 large eggs
Nutmeg, salt, pepper to taste
8 small egg yolks
¼ lb. butter
Grated Romano cheese minced Italian parsley, for garnish

ALRIGHT: Long as you got a pasta machine, this one ain't so bad for all you freshpasta-phobics. Kind of almost like playing advanced sand-castle building.

First let's get those tomatoes reconstituted and well-rinsed; and let's do the same for your fancy mushrooms—soaking them in warm water for about half an hour; rinsing; discard-ing stems and cutting into thin strips. Also look back to the introductory chapter to figure out how to put together a quick pasta dough.

Now let's mix up, stir, smoosh up our special stuffing in a large bowl: the ricotta, the Romano, the two large eggs, the reconstituted tomatoes ground up in a food processor or fine-chopped. Add and mix in your salt, pepper with the Italian touch of fresh-grated nutmeg.

Next step: Roll out your pasta up to setting #5 and cut in 10" strips (about 10" times 4½" rectangles). So that the pasta won't stick lay the rectangles on floured sheets of parchment on a large tray or pan. Then place the stuffing into a pastry bag and pipe silver dollar circles onto the middle of one-half of each 10" pasta sheet; drop a small egg yolk into each circle and neatly fold the empty half of the pasta rectangle over the top of the stuffing side. Then carefully cut out your circular tortelli with a four-inch cookie-cutter. Trim the edges with your hands, then feather-brush the edges with water to prevent leakage and seal/crimp the edges with a pasta cutter. You can refriger-ate until ready to use.

Flour brush the tortellis—don't worry, the flour will go away in the water. Then slide (don't drop them in, stupido—slide it like you're going to poach an egg) them into a pot of salted water at a slow boil. Then turn the water up a little for 3-5 minutes.

Meanwhile, let's melt our stick of butter in a skillet and sauté our reconstituted mushies. We're getting our butter brown (NOT BURNED) so that it's close to caramelized. Then you can spoon half the butter into individual dishes as a base for the pasta. Best way to test the pasta is to break off a stray little piece and taste it with your dentees, honey. Remove with large spoons and onto butter from mushrooms—two per serving would probably be right. Then heap the mushrooms and remaining butter over the tortellis and sprinkle on your ever faithful Romano. Italian—non-curly—parsley is your special garnish—and GOD help you, it'll taste so good. That potato/veggie pizza will be great to lap up every last drop of mushroom flavored butter on your plate. ■

40 SECOND DESSERT

1 cup mascarpone cheese
¼ cup whipping cream
½ tsp. vanilla
1 tsp. honey
2 cups fresh raspberries
Fresh, grated nutmeg, for garnish

WELL, maybe Chef Carl was dreaming of balmy winters in Pontiac, Michigan when he made up this title. Maybe it'll be 5 or 10 minutes for us mere mortals. But it is simple. Let's just whip up the mascarpone with the whipping cream as thinner, adding our dashes of vanilla and honey. Into a piping bag.

Raspberries—about half a cup per plate. Pipe about two tablespoons of the cream onto each portion of the berries. Just a wee dash of fresh grated nutmeg and you're done. Not a world record but close enough to get Chef Carl's honorable mention. ■

CHAPTER EIGHT

This is Carl's great unpizza show and he's making a veggie stew which will be a great accompaniment to the meatloaf that's the, kinda, main dish. The only pizza feature will be a crust for the Meatloaf Italian (or Meatloaf Wellington if you're hot on limeys). The stew can be prepared a day or two before serving and the meatloaf itself could be prepared in advance and served cold like a pâté. The super rich Zabaglione can be made very quickly so you'll be able to take it relatively easy before your dinner guests arrive.

VEGGIE STEW

2	red bell peppers
4	Tb. olive oil
½	lb. asparagus, chopped in ½″ pieces
1	zucchini, sliced
5	celery stalks, sliced
1	large red onion, fine-chopped
2	medium carrots, sliced
¾	cup Italian parsley leaves, fine-chopped
1	28 oz.-can Italian plum tomatoes, squeezed dry
1	cup chicken stock (or broth)
½	tsp. each marjoram & oregano
¼	tsp. each pepper & salt
¼	cup grated pecorino Romano cheese

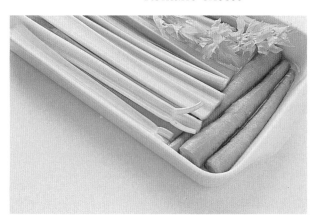

HERE'S a true prima vera vegetable dish for those of you trying to cut out the meat a little (though Carl does include it in this Chapter as an accompaniment to the special meatloaf he's about to describe). Start by preparing two steam-roasted red (or yellow or even green, depending on what's available) bell peppers as you did in Chap. 3 and peeling, slicing them and then halving the slices.

Meanwhile slice your celery, carrots and zucchini and chop your asparagus. Then take out your trusty mezzaluna (half moon, huh, Guiseppe?) and fine chop your onion and parsley.

Now heat 4 tablespoons of Carl's old standby olive oil in a large skillet and introduce the multicolor of the veggies to the light sizzle of a medium heat, stirring occasionally for 5 minutes. De-seed the tomatoes (you've squeezed them dry already in paper towels) through a mill and add them to the skillet, followed by the stock (use supermarket broth if you must—but it'll probably be salty). Season to taste. Carl says it's your choice.

Stir, then turn to simmer for a half-hour or so and let the mix thicken as vegetables kind of soften and pick up each other's spring/summer flavors. About a quarter of an hour through the simmer, stir in the grated pecorino and you're picking up a truly Italian tang. Again, you can serve it hot or cold (Carl maybe just about prefers it cold) as a great side dish for the Italian Meatloaf Wellington on the very next page, cuore mio. Cut that spicy meatloaf (or you could have it with a sausage). Spike it on to your fork, smother it with this more sauce than stew, and let your dentees taste il paradisio. ■

ITALIAN MEATLOAF

1	lb. pizza dough
2	slices white bread
2	cups red wine
20	basil leaves
½	cup parsley
2	cloves garlic
2	lb. top of the round beef (or pre-ground)
1	lb. Italian Sausage—sweet
4	large eggs
¾	lb. Prosciutto, sliced thin
½	lb. smoked mozzarella cheese
3	oz. sun-dried tomatoes (reconstituted: soaked in water and squeeze-dried)
¾	cup flour for dusting meatloaf

A BIG dish—not quite so easy, so pay attention—for which Chef Carl became Honorable Member Fraternal Order Detroit Sons of Italy along with Night Train Lane, Gordie Howe and Mrs. Henry Ford Jrs. 1, 2 and 3. Italian Meatloaf—cugino to Beef Wellington—with a crust of pizza dough. On the TV show, Carl was slightly nonplused by having to use an old-fashioned meat grinder for his beef and sausage—that gestapo agent of a lady producer trying to make him stay away from electronic gadgetry to keep the audience in the Dakotas. But you could even buy some ground meat and smoosh the seasoning in.

Start by preparing your basic pizza dough two or three hours ahead of time. Now take your 2 slices of white bread (Carl actually used an equivalent chunk—2 oz.—of Muffuletta bread from Show 4), break them up, and mix with a cup of the red wine (not "cooking wine"— use the real thing) over a medium heat. You're creating a kind of roux, a paste, to work into the meatloaf. So you're stirring, smooshing, pressing the bread and wine into a paste. As the bread begins to dissolve, turn the heat to simmer—and as it melds turn the durn thing off and let it cool its heels.

Now we're ready for that 1940s meat grinder (or your processor or you can just get the ground round if you're bone idle) and Carl actually puts 10 basil leaves, the parsley, the garlic through the grinder along with the top of the round and finocchio—sweetened Italian sausage—but smoosh it all together if meat is pre-ground.

This meat mix you can place in a baking dish with 2″ sides. Add the wine/bread roux and press it all down.

Move the meat mix to one side of the baking dish and drop and beat the eggs in the other side. Now work the meat and eggs—your binding agent—together and press it all down throughout the dish as you add a final cup of wine to this aristocratic meatloaf mix.

PHASE 2: Now we take our ¾ pound of very thin-sliced Prosciutto—Carl counts 24 of them for this attempt. Lay them out, slightly overlapping each other, into a pattern about 18″ by 12″. On top of the Prosciutto, lay out your smoked mozzarella slices in similar fashion (notice that Carl hasn't put salt in his meatloaf—that will come from these two ingredients). Now lay out your reconstituted California sun-dried tomatoes (less salty than those shipped over from Italia) on top of the smoked mozzarella and scatter the remaining basil leaves across your field of play.

Right: Now things get just a little tricky; but just keep your cool and you'll have la buona fortuna: rub your hands with a little olive oil so that things don't get sticky. Now place the meatloaf into the middle of the Prosciutto/mozzarella layout and wrap the sides and ends of said layout over the top of the meatloaf. Now you want to truss this affair much as you would tie up a salami. Slip some kitchen string (about 5 times the length of the meatloaf) under and around the thing lengthwise; cross over and loop around the side in the middle

(well—see the illustration) and at both ends so that you end up with only one knot to be cut when you're ready.

So take your meatloaf in bondage, thinly coat it in flour and sauté it in 3 or 4 tablespoons of olive oil, using large spatulas to lift it if you don't have a kitchen crane. After about 4 minutes, turn the thing over with your spatulas and do the other side. So—the eggs have coagulated a little, cheese melted, juices are sealed. Remove the meatloaf (can we call it simply that anymore?) and place on lightly oiled parchment. Cut the knot, Alexi—and set your meatloaf free.

BIG STEP: Roll out your pound of dough into a square of about 18″ sides. Into a large steel baking pan with 1½″ sides that is lightly oiled, lay silicon parchment paper, and lay the dough on top of this with sides hanging over the pan. Now place the meatloaf into the center of the dough and fold ends and then sides over the meat. Tuck flaps in and try to get the seams underneath so that the weight of the thing is pushing down for securement. Let the monster sit for, say, 15 minutes so that the dough will get a little volume, a little puffy.

Final stage: Into the oven, preheated at 375°F., onto the stone for about 25-35 minutes until a LIGHT golden brown. Let cool some and then slice with a sharp or serated knife. Serve a slice or two heaped with your veggie stew and your local Junior League will be begging you for demonstrations. ∎

ZABAGLIONE

4	egg yolks
1	cup sugar
½	cup Marsala (or equivalent wine)

FOR this simple but super rich and famous dessert, you'll need a double boiler, or some kind of bowl sitting on not quite boiling water. Start off with your four large egg yolks at room temperature—Carl likes to separate them the way he saw his demi-idol Jacques Pépin do it—just cracks them all into a bowl and separates them with his hands and fingers. No need for gadgets, here. So egg yolks in the double boiler. Begin to beat the eggs, making sure that the water doesn't get too hot and thus cooking the eggs into scrambled, and gradually beat in your sugar and your wine tablespoon by tablespoon. The trick is to just keep beating away—if it looks like the eggs are in danger of congealing, just remove the saucepan or bowl. What we're aiming at is a thin custard or hollandaise consistency. Keep it moving. Should take about 5 minutes of beating to approach the right stage—won't just pour fast off the whisk. Then spoon the custard into, say, wine glasses and garnish with a strawberry on the edge of the glass. Could use this as an excellent sauce to maybe a pound cake—your choice, PIZZA GOURMET. ■

CHAPTER NINE

Aren't you so impressed that Carl the Detroit Pole can be so, well, Italianate with the cuisine?

So take a giant gasp of amazement and witness el Carl the Sheik, no less, with an array of dishes from the near and dear East—didn't we say in our opening invocation to this epic paradiso of pizza/pasta that maybe the original pizza came from the East like the mozzarella from the water buffalo? Our sheik will swoop down to your counter with tasty Hummus to be dipped into with Pita Bread which can also swoosh up the Tabouli he'll show-you-how-to-make. Then Lahmajoon and Armenian pizzas—with special Eastern meats and a special way to toast. ■

PITA	4-6	cups all-purpose flour
BREAD	1½	cups water
	1½	tsp. dry yeast
	1	tsp. salt
	2	tsp. olive oil

LIKE the Italians, who use the bread to sop up the gravy or the last of the homemade tomato sauce, in, say, Lebanon, the bread is used maybe more than knives and forks. Carl makes a similar bread to that which the old Armenian ladies up in Detroit make—though he sort of likes to use his old standby olive oil to make sure of the elasticity and they don't. And the little old ladies stay with a sheet of steel for their bread while he sticks with his stone.

So Carl is going to use the basic non-gadget way of making pizza to create the pocket bread of the East. So we'll create a well of flour, again. We'll end up using 4-6 cups of flour, but the precise amount of flour is less important than the amount of liquid we'll use. So with the fork we'll gradually stir in the water; stir in our yeast, let the bubbles start, add in our salt, our olive oil, let it get to the same stage as the dough we made in the intro.

Then into a bowl and cover with a dish towel and set at room temperature. While we let the pizza dough rise for a con-siderably longer time, pita bread dough only really needs maybe an hour and a half before you can roll it out and stick it in the oven.

Divide the dough into six-ounce pieces and roll them out individually. Roll out the individual pieces of dough and set them on the peel which once more should be well blessed with cornmeal. Set them on the stone in the 375-400 degree oven for about ten minutes—until they puff and their tops take on a light brownish color—let them rise in the oven without having played around with them too much. Remove them while they're still nice and soft, set them on a rack and cover them with a towel so that they stay soft until you're ready to start sopping with them. ∎

HUMMUS

1   lb. canned garbanzo beans
1   cup Tahini sauce
1-1½ cups olive oil
2   cloves garlic, chopped
     Salt & pepper to taste
¼   cup lemon juice
     Mint leaves and Cayenne
     pepper, for garnish

SO here's one quick and easy spread to go with your PITA Bread—you can make it while the bread's in the oven. We're going to use a food processor, but you could use a blender, or, like the folks in the old country, you could use a pestle & mortar gig. Carl got his Tahini from a natural food store, but you could even make that by roasting, say, four cups of sesame seeds in the oven at 350 for 8-10 minutes and blend them or grind them with ½ cup of safflower or vegetable oil. And you could soak and boil the garbanzo beans. But we're going quick and easy.

So we put our gabanzos, Tahini and oil into the processor and run for about five seconds—perhaps purists might not use the oil, but Carl likes the smooth texture it, uh, yields. Then two chopped cloves of garlic and, if you want, a little salt—maybe half a teaspoon plus a couple shakes of pepper and your lemon juice. Carl likes real lemon juice—not the juice from the bottle, so he rolls it around on the counter to loosen up the juice and make it easier to remove the pips. Squeeze it in a fist through your fingers and the pips will just remain in your hand. Then blend for about 45 seconds more adding maybe another half cup of oil if consistency is not yet smooth enough.

Pour this creamy mixture onto an oval plate, garnish around the edges with mint leaves, sprinkle lightly with cayenne pepper and maybe one more teaspoon of oil in the center for a true presentation AND get with da Pita Bread! ■

TABOULI

1½ cups Bulgur Wheat
3 cups water
3 cups tomatoes, chopped
½ cup cucumber, chopped
1 8 oz.-can garbanzo beans
1 head—2 cups—curly parsley
½ cup mint
1—2 garlic cloves
¼ cup lemon juice
½ cup olive oil
 Salt & pepper to taste
2 Tb. cinammon
 Parsley, for garnish

THIS is a second, wheat-based appetizer—the kind that you can fit in the pocket of the bread and smear a little with the Hummus—or you could serve with lettuce leaves as the bread equivalent. You can really put in this dish what you like, whatever is available at certain times of the year, like they'd do back in the old country. Carl's going to use tomatoes, parsley, mint, garbanzos, cukes, etc., but you could use bell peppers and green onions—to each his own, Luigi.

So we'll start by soaking the bulgur in the water for two hours. Meanwhile we'll start fine-chopping our tomatoes and placing them in a large bowl. Peel and chop the cuke, then fine-chop it with a mezzaluna and add to bowl. Then add the soaked and expanded bulgur and the garbanzos to the mix.

Chop and mezzaluna both the parsley and the mint, then fine-chop the garlic and add to the bulgur mixture. Now add the lemon juice, using the same technique that Carl uses for the lemon in the Hummus. Then stir in the oil and dash of salt and pepper to taste. Just for that special Eastern effect, let's add a coupla tablespoons of cinnamon and we're ready for the well-mixed bowl to be spooned onto, say, a square platter garnished around with sprigs of the unitalian, curley parsley. ∎

LAHMAJOON

18 oz. pizza dough
1 lb. fine-ground shoulder of lamb
¼ cup Italian parsley, chopped
1 Tb. fresh mint, fine-chopped
2 cloves garlic, fine-chopped
2 Tb. olive oil
1 large onion, chopped fine
1 small green bell pepper, fine-chopped
1 tsp. each salt & pepper
1 Tb. cinnamon
1 cup canned Italian plum tomatoes
4 Tb. tomato paste
¼ cup roasted pine nuts (optional)
Olive oil, to brush

SO this is Carl's version of the Eastern Lahmajoon: a no-cheese pizza that Carl usually sees prepared with small fried egg-size dough that's folded over the filling and stacked high until ready for re-warming. Again, you've got to go with what's available—might, f'rinstance want to mix fresh rosemary in with the lamb. And the ground lamb itself might not be so easy to find, though if there's a good butcher around you should be OK. Carl himself wasn't able to find shoulder the other day when he shot for TV. So he found some lamb chops to grind up (sans bone)— grinding in the parsley, mint and garlic with the lamb.

So you'll prepare your 18 oz. or slightly more of dough, and, before ready to roll, divide into six pieces. Mix lamb, spices and garlic. Meanwhile sauté the fine-chopped onion in an olive-oiled skillet. Add the chopped bell pepper, then the ground lamb with spicing mixed in. Stir in the salt, pepper, and cinnamon and let the meat lightly brown—the pink hardly gone, it will cook more in the oven. Now cool the mix down by adding the tomatoes that have been drained and then dried in a dish towel and chopped. Then stir in the tomato paste and, if you want to get super-Eastern, a quarter cup of roasted pine nuts.

Now roll out three pieces of dough—about six ounces each— until thin (especially in the center—press down with your hands if you must). Build up the edges to at least a quarter of an inch high crust so that the juices will be contained— remember, we don't have our cheese binding. The edge will expand in the oven. Lift the rings of dough onto the old cornmealed peel and spread about a cup of filling onto each piece. Make sure again that the crust is built up a little and poke the center to prevent rising. Slide onto the stone at 500°F. for 15-20 minutes—until the edges are golden brown and the bottom edge is warped. Out onto a drying rack, brush the edges with olive oil and you're set to eat with the sheik.

ARMENIAN PIZZA

1 lb. pizza dough
Olive oil to brush
8 oz. mozzarella cheese, diced
3 oz. pastema
3 oz. soojouk
2 fresh plum tomatoes
4 oz. kasseri cheese

HERE'S a short something to round out our Eastern theme. It'll tend to depend, Ali, on whether you can get hold of an Armenian sausage—soojouk, usually beef-based—and pastema—hunks from the rib area of beef that is salted, soaked, marinated in a spice mixture of chaimen, and then hung up to age. Well, use your imagination, or call your friendly Lebanese hairdresser.

So roll out your square pizza and slide onto peel. Brush with olive oil and spread the glue, the diced mozzarella. Slice your soojouk and pastema and ring the outside of the dough with them in alternate slices. Then line the inside of the meat ring with sliced tomatoes and arrange other slices across the middle. Sprinkle on your kasseri and onward to the oven stone at the regular 500°F. for fifteen minutes and you've got a desert gold delight to whisk away onto the cooling rack. Then oil the edges.

Simple enough? Let's celebrate our successful negotiations by adding a drop of water to a shot of licorice/ouzo-like ARAK and down the milky way before we dip into the hummus.

CHAPTER TEN

OK, so maybe you think you've gotten past that pizza cadet level; maybe you think you've arrived at journeyman gastronaut, as Carl's English admiree, Mr. Floyd on Fish, might say in a fleeting moment of sobriety. Well, let's check it out—we'll try out a couple of the tricks that Carl has shown you in new dishes. We'll work those roasted bell peppers from Chapter 3 into a scampi and make a dessert variation of calzone, too. So, since Carl has been cruising the bayous and bays around N'Orlins, LA, we'll try out some quick and half-fast shellfish combos—right, Boudreaux, mon ami? We'll start with a couple of appetizers that you can sop up with your focaccia, change pace with spinach pasta, then grand slam with one of old Carl's premier, top-of-the line, grand-slam pizzas. Mean to say: this is a pizza book, no? ■

SCAMPI	1	each, green, red, yellow large bell peppers, roasted (see Chapter 3)
	4	Tb. melted butter
	2	Tb. chopped garlic
	2	Tb. chopped parsley
	2	lb. medium shrimp in shells, (remove heads)
SAUCE	¾	cup ketchup
	2	Tb. horseradish sauce
		Juice of 1 lemon
		Dash Worcestershire sauce
		Dash Tabasco sauce

SCAMPI, you know, is Italian for shrimp or prawns—plural for "scampo"—so there ain't a "Shrimp Scampi" anymore than there's a "pizza pie" or an automobile motor-car.

But, anyway, remember those peppers from Chapter 3: turning them in the oven, wrapped in a dish with plastic wrap, soaked in iced water and the skins stripped off? Well, let's do the same again with one green, one yellow and one red pepper. Cut the skinned peppers into thin strips. Set aside.

Now let's find some medium-size fresh whole shrimp—that's it, shells, head and all—if you can find them, rather than the frozen kind you'll get in supermarkets. Since this is going to be an appetizer that people will dunk in a dip before eating, try not to get them too large or people will want to dunk a shrimp more than once in the dip and that's not too genteel, now.

In a skillet, heat butter and 2 tablespoons of chopped garlic (maybe from your garlic and oil jar) over a medium heat. Now add shrimp to the skillet. You don't want the shrimp peeled, now, or they'll become too saturated by the garlic—too heavy a flavor—let your guests peel them if they want to. Switch the heat up when you add the shrimp. When the shrimp turn pink and their little tails curl up, they're done. Now pour the shrimp onto your standard oval platter and at one end and two sides begin your presentation by placing three large leaves—maybe giant broccoli leaves—stem under shrimp, leaf outward. Now mix your pepper strips into the shrimp and play with the colors.

For some cocktail sauce, mix a teaspoon of horseradish sauce into the ketchup. Add lemon juice and Worcestershire sauce and Tabasco. Pour this into a small glass bowl and find a place for it on your platter—maybe at the unleafed end or just where you want, really. Now sprinkle your chopped parsley over both sauce and scampi. One spoonful of horseradish in the center of the sauce and you're all set. Well, maybe a bowl to discard the shrimp shells and protect your new carpet. ∎

CRAWFISH
LAGNIAPPE

1 stick (¼ lb.) butter
⅓ cup chopped garlic
1 Tb. olive oil
1 tsp. marjoram
1 lb. package boiled crawfish tails
1 tsp. black pepper
Dash each of Worcestershire and Tabasco sauce
Garnish:
2 whole crawfish, boiled; kale leaves, savoy cabbage flower

HERE'S another little appetizer that Carl presents from Luzanne. Remember, though, that they're breeding crawfish (crayfish to you snobs, crawdaddies to hippies and crackers) all over the country. Carl's gonna use precooked and packaged, though still good, crawfish tails; but he'll save a few whole boiled crawfish for presentation. We'll use a lot of butter because we're gonna sop up the sauce with focaccia. Melt your butter in a skillet and add garlic (Carl has his own little electric garlic chopper for convenience). You can have a high heat, and add olive oil and marjoram. Then add your bag of crawfish tails, black pepper, Worcestershire and Tabasco sauce. As the crawfish are already boiled, cooking time is only about two minutes. Pour onto your oval platter and garnish at one end with maybe kale and the purple flower of a savoy cabbage. At the other end, place two whole boiled crawfish (they're like pygmy lobsters) and you have a superfast appetizer.

Both the scampi and the crawfish can go with focaccia (see Chapter 12). For a change, though, you might try using roasted shallots (halfway between garlic and onion) instead of the roasted garlic. So sop away and let's move onto heavier sitting things. ■

SPINACH LASAGNE

1	Tb. olive oil
10	peeled, whole cloves of garlic for sauce
10	plum tomatoes
20	oz. ricotta cheese
1	Tb. Romano cheese
3	Tb. butter
	Pinch fresh grated nutmeg
1½	cups fresh spinach leaves
	Salt for boiling
1	lb. Pasta Dough
18	fresh basil leaves
10	oz. mozzarella cheese, diced

NOW to return to our red, white and green eye-talian design with some homemade spinach lasagne—Popeye goes pasta. How else to start but by brushing a skillet with olive oil? Sauté 10 whole, peeled cloves of garlic and add tomatoes. When the tomatoes are heated and softened, put them through a food mill after removing most of the garlic cloves because we want this sauce to be real delicate. Carl just gets angry at the thought of those acidy seeds and skins and turns his handle even harder. The sauce he's looking for should be a little bit orange. If it's red, they've used tomato paste—ugh! And maybe sweetened it with sugar. No thank you. Back in the skillet and let it simmer down 'til you're ready.

Now prepare for another layer: with your ricotta, Romano, butter and fresh-grated nutmeg and smoosh it up roughly. Meanwhile boil water with about 2 tablespoons of salt added and add the spinach, bringing it just back to the boil. The salt will preserve the fresh greenness of the spinach. Then take the spinach, via a colander, put in iced water then squeeze out the water. You should end up with about half a cup of boiled spinach which you can chop up. Add the spinach to your pasta dough just as it's beginning to get porridgy. Run the dough through the pasta machine until its finest setting, as you'd do for Fettucine Alfredo except don't cut fettucine for this dish (reserve some of the pieces for crawfish fettucine, however). You should cut the pasta into lengths of 6-8." Boil the pasta for about 30 seconds in salted water and dip into iced water to stop the cooking process.

Now brush a baking dish about 12″ x 8″ x 2″ with olive oil and lay down your first layer of pasta to cover not merely the bottom and sides of the dish but to have about a 1″ to 1½″ overhang around the edge. Splash on a layer of sauce and place basil leaves on top for seasoning. Then place your second layer of pasta—but no overhang is necessary except for that bottom one. Next a layer of your ricotta mix which you can press down with the third pasta cover. Now a layer of your mozzarella. And now the last layer of pasta which can be topped with another layer of sauce with basil leaves sprinkled over. Now take that overhang from the bottom layer of pasta and fold it back over the inside edges of the dish. Place the dish on a rack about 6″ over the stone with the oven at 375-400°F. for about 25 minutes (remember, the pasta has already been boiled). Let it cool for 10 minutes or so and slice it up. ■

As another lagniappe, let's make some fettucine from the fine spinach pasta noodles you made, before they get too dry, but add a few sun-dried tomatoes and half a pound of the boiled crawfish tails to a pasta dish over a pot of boiling water before you boil the noodles and add them to the dish. Haven't got any more crawfish? Try some lobster or even shrimp. Maybe heat the mix in a skillet for awhile as you stir to thicken. Serve on an oval platter with a sprinkle of Romano and a couple of whole crawfish at one end for presentation and you've got a great addition to the appetizers, the lasagne and the seafood pizza that you're about to build, shipmates.

SEAFOOD PIZZA

1 lb. pizza dough
  Garlic and oil for brushing
¼ lb. mozzarella cheese, diced
¾ lb. shrimp, peeled and deveined
  Large black pitted olives (1 per shrimp)
4 fresh plum (Roma) tomatoes, thin-sliced
⅛ lb. bel paese cheese
¼ lb. goat's cheese or gorgonzola cheese
4 strips raw bacon, sliced into 1″ or 2″ pieces
  Romano cheese to sprinkle

WELL, well—another top of the line pizza using 1 lb. of your basic dough however you want to make it, machine or hand. No sauce on this either.

OK we roll, punch and stretch our dough out to just under the paddle size. And, but of course, we scatter cornmeal across our peel. Let's brush the dough with garlic and oil after we've transferred dough to peel and then put diced mozzarella across dough with just an inch margin for crust. Now let's place the shrimp symmetrically around pizza and put a black olive in the center of each shrimp—in its curl. Intersperse tomato slices between shrimp and maybe line the two ends of the pizza also with tomato slices. Now scatter drops of the bel paese and goat's cheese (or gorgonzola) around—don't worry, the cheese will melt down to a uniform position. Also, let's work the small strips of bacon into the design, then brush each shrimp with garlic and oil and the pizza is ready for blessing to make sure it'll move off the peel. Then it's back to the back of the stone at your angle, jerk the peel back towards you and let it sit in there at the old 500 until the bottom edges begin to warp and we're all set to enjoy with another brushing of the crust with oil and a sprinkle of Romano. And, uh, dolce far niente, dolce far niente… ∎

**STRAW-
BERRIES
AND
PEACHES
CALZONE**

1 16 oz. package cream
   cheese
1½ cups ricotta cheese
6 fresh strawberries
2 ripe peaches
   Basic pizza dough rolled
   out and divided by 3″
   cookie cutter
1 8 oz. can chocolate sauce
1½ cups fresh blueberries
⅓ cup blueberry preserves
1 2 oz. bar of milk chocolate
   for shavings
12 fresh raspberries and sprigs
   of mint, for garnish

WELL, maybe one final lagniappe if you've passed the test. Remember that Calzone Delight that you made in Chapter 1? Or check the 5-Cheese Calzone in Chapter 12. Remember the regular pizza dough, remember the cookie cutter? Remember Mrs. What-Was-Her Name's wallpaper sealer for the second seal and the pinch and braiding technique for the final seal? Well, we'll use the same method for a dessert calzone. We'll use cream cheese and ricotta—yes, your old versatile ricotta can work

for all sorts of combinations: it's a binder, really. Mix the cream cheese and ricotta up, smoosh them well. Slice the FRESH strawberries (nothing frozen, thank you, no excess moisture) and dice the fresh, ripe peaches. Now add the strawberries to the outside top of the smooshed cheese ball. Now take three thick dobs of strawberries and cheese—maybe a quarter cup each—and put them in the middle of three of your cut out dough circles. Now repeat the process with your diced peaches. So you'll end up with three and three. Now make your three seals and slice the tops for venting. Place them on a tray with parchment covering and put on the stone at 500 degrees for 10-15 minutes—until golden brown.

Meanwhile, back at the range, heat the chocolate sauce. In another saucepan heat the blueberries (or raspberries, or...) with preserves on a high heat. Squash them down and strain them for a pure sauce. So we have two sauces either of which can go with either of the calzones. Shave some chocolate from a bar for garnish.

Now the calzones should be ready. Place each calzone on the side of a separate plate. Pour some sauce to the side of the calzone so that the rest of the plate is covered with sauce. Now place fresh raspberries around the far edge of the plate. Sprinkle chocolate shavings over both sauce and calzone and maybe a sprig of mint in center of sauce. Would a little powdered sugar make it all too decadent? That's up to you.

And thanks, again, Mrs. Richards. ■

81

CHAPTER ELEVEN

Just as that old pasta twirler Galileo Galilei must have rolled over from his sleep one early Italian dawn to reckon that maybe the sun didn't revolve around the earth like a pizza pie, so it has come upon Chef Carlo that, "You could use fruit on pizza." Just take your mind off the tomato sauce and you'll discover a universe of possibility. Chef Carlo wants to present you with a veritable Olympic opening ceremony march past a United Nations flag display of toppings. So let's change pizza direction in mid-air spin, as it were, and go from dinner party to breakfast or brunch. What, you say, maybe il padrone has been too long in the Dearborn, Michigan sun today? Well, now, just expand your mind to the possibilities of la dolce pizzeria. ■

GOOD MORNING PIZZA

1	medium red onion, thin-sliced
¾	cup mushrooms, sliced
1	green pepper, thin-sliced in circles
	Flowers of two small broccoli stalks, chopped
2	Tb. garlic
2	Tb. vegetable (olive) oil
1	lb. basic pizza dough
½	stick butter, melted
5	large eggs
4	oz. cheddar cheese, grated
4	oz. mozzarella cheese, grated
1	small zucchini, sliced
	Salt and pepper to taste
	Grated Romano cheese

THIS is a GOOD MORNING PIZZA. Listen—you watch the late news? Hey, prepare your basic dough while you listen to who just got arrested for bribery or obstruction of justice—it'll be ready in the morning. So let's thin-slice our onion, mushrooms, green pepper and maybe some broccoli. (Carl didn't plan on the broccoli for his show, but in his own existential/compulsive way just had to when the director called "action." Sauté the veggies in garlic and oil—gives 'em a nice flavor—over medium heat.

Now let's flour our board and roll out the dough (again, best to mark out the dimensions on your surface so that the dough won't be too big for your oven stone or peel). Put square dough on the peel and brush the dough not with your standard dinner pizza olive oil but with melted butter, again though, as a moisture barrier.

Now beat 4 of the eggs (always try to bring them to room temperature before cooking) lightly in a bowl and add your diced cheeses (could use cheeses of your choice, it's up to you, Ricci, but Carl likes the yellow cheddars or colbys on account of the yellows bringing out the eggs). So mix together your egg/cheese and spread it across your dough, maybe leaving a 2 by 3 inch space in the middle because that's the part that doesn't cook just quite so well. Now spread the sautéed vegetables over the cheese/egg mix, placing one green pepper ring for the middle gap. Now place the raw zucchini slices around the edge of the pizza. And listen! You or your picky friend don't like zucchini? Use something else—pepperoni, bacon, Italian sausage. Once Carl couldn't find any zucchini in the stores, so guess what: he used a cucumber! Everyone thought it was great. One day, Carl plans to try topping this off with a fresh strawberry puree. You try it first, send him a letter, Fed Ex, and tell him how it was.

Now for a cute little trick up Carl's sleeve with all the others: Maybe you've been scratching your head that you've only used 4 of your 5 eggs. So, drop a raw egg into that center pepper ring! Sneak up on your guests with an egg in some dark late night corner and you'll catch 'em— it's real showy. Make sure that pizza moves! Give it the cornmeal blessing if it sticks somewhere. Now take it to the back of the stone at your maybe 30° angle and give it that jerk towards you. If a little dough hangs over the stone just push it back on with the tip of your peel. Bake 10-15 minutes at your basic 500°F. The bottom edges of your pizza should begin to warp a little—an uneven bottom crust—showing that your good moanin' is ready. Now Carl likes to put his gourmet pizza on a drying rack so that the flat surface of a counter won't create steam to make the pizza soggy again. A little melted butter around the edges, some Romano sprinkled across your, may Carl say, pizza artist's canvas, let it cool awhile and you're set for a breakfast, brunch, midnight snack, or whatever, that would create oohs and ahs even at the Guggenheim administrative staff cafeteria. ∎

FRUITZA	1	lb. pizza dough
CHEESE	½	stick butter, melted
PIZZA	15	oz. ricotta cheese
	½	cup cream cheese
	½	cup sugar
	2	tsp. cinnamon
	½	cup raisins
	2	large baking apples (e.g. Roma or Granny Smith), unpeeled but cored and sliced—about 9 slices)
	1	banana, sliced
	1-2	sliced kiwis
	2	oz. chocolate chips
	12	fresh strawberries, sliced and 1 whole strawberry
	½	cup raspberry preserves
	1	Tb. powdered sugar

SO, since we've just made a Good Morning Pizza let's keep going off on the same tangent and make a truly delicious dessert of a FRUIT PIZZA. Crazy, you say. Let Chef Carlo repeat that pizza is pizza as long as you don't do something like sweetening the dough with butter. Then pizza is not pizza. But if you use the regular dough, then it's fun to see what you can make out of something that maybe seems a little bland before you start building the old edible artwork.

So let's roll out the regular pound of dough and onto your cornmealed paddle, brush it with melted butter. And let's mix in a bowl the ricotta, cream cheese, sugar, cinnamon and raisins. Don't like raisins? Leave them out. Put in what you want. Put maybe nine dollops of the mix, ordered like a tic tac toe game around the pizza and press a slice of apple over each one. Then spread the banana across the pizza around the outskirts of the apple/cheese rings. Banana can take the heat! Now let's make sure that the pizza can move on the peel and bless it if it won't (you're tired of hearing that? Well maybe we lay off it for a couple chapters). Angle the peel back, jerk back towards you—and bake 10-15 minutes at 500°F. When bottom edges begin to warp then bring it out on a rack and let's start to give it some color 'cause it looks kinda bland now.

So butter the edge with your brush and how about spreading some kiwi around to start off Carl's Pizza of Many Colours, Jackson? And how about some chocolate chips while it's still hot enough to melt them? The pizza will steam the fresh fruit a little too, though they and the chocolate would be spoiled under the intense heat of the oven and stone. So lay on the fresh sliced strawberries, MacDuff—and fresh raspberries too if you want—a great Christmas brunch, no? Let's line the inside of the crust with raspberry preserves and put a small dollop (or fresh raspberry) in the holed center of each apple. A fresh strawberry in the middle, sprinkle powdered sugar as a final garnish and it's nirvana hot or cold. ∎

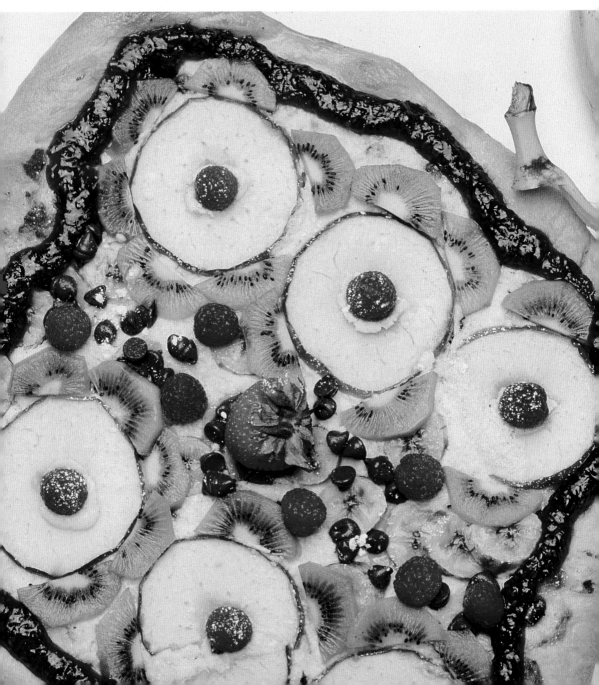

PASTA
KUGEL

¼ lb. butter
Salt for boiling noodles
10 oz. fettucine noodles
8 large eggs
1 cup ricotta cheese
1 cup sour cream
½ cup raisins
⅓ cup sugar
2 Tb. cinnamon

NOW going right along in that same brunch/dessert vein, Carl Oshinsky, pontiff of pizza and pasta prince, has a little something that he might delicately say is very Jewish. Matter of fact, Carl adapted this Pasta Kugel from one of those recipes that his old mum, down in Florida now,

will give to her son as he drives along, with her in the back seat, on the way from the airport. Not a pizza maker herself, she'll tell you, yet, that kugel is a kind of cake, pie made with eggs, matza flour and grated potatoes or maybe noodles. With noodles, it's Lukschen Kugel—so maybe back in Brooklyn in the long ago your friendly Italiano was your friendly Luksh. Instead of the old wide noodles his mama cooked, Carl likes to use that slender fettucine that he made himself in Chapter 12—gives it such a light touch, almost like a fine bread pudding—hardly even know the noodles are there.

Now on top of a large pot of boiling water, melt your butter in a dish. Then salt the water—no oil—and add your pasta. Drain the noodles in your colander. Now let's break the eggs into the melted butter and heat them slightly before adding the ricotta, sour cream, raisins, sugar and cinnamon. Smoosh, maybe with a large spoon. Now put the mix into a porcelain or metal baking dish, about three inches deep. The oven should go down to about 375°F. for this and you should have a metal rack, maybe an inch over the stone. Bake about 30-40 minutes (Carl isn't going to lie to you: no oven's the same), check for that golden brown top that's risen and you'll have something sweet and fine to go with your Good Morning or Fruitza Pizza. Let it cool and serve warm or cold, even. ■

CORNUCOPIA AND FRUIT TABLE

NOW for a slightly less edible work of art. Well, you can eat it if you just can't resist its elegant lines, but the cornucopia, Chef Carl's veritable horn of plenty, will set off this menu by being the feature attraction for the fruit table that rounds out these sweet delights.

Well, let's get in the groove with our basic pizza dough (see Introduction), only this time we'll add a little sugar, just a teaspoon to the messy mix. What we want to arrive at is a less wet, more crumbly/flaky piece of dough, stiffer too, with a drop more salt and more flour. Let your processor, or tender hands, tighten it up. After you've got your tennis ball effect, add more flour until you've got a stodgy/sturdy porridge-like dough. Knead it on your floured board (using the old clockwise

Carl likes to, you know, negotiate a little at the florist—asks, "Got any broken stems…"—he's gonna break the stems anyway. "Maybe a few discarded fern leaves?"

By the way, don't buy greens and veggies that are packed on ice—means they're getting old and will wilt in your car.

folding movement) until it's tight, then set it aside to rise for just about an hour.

While it's rising, let's make our mold of plenty (actually of aluminum foil and parchment). Now listen, Luksh! Don't make your horn too big for your oven. No three foot horn for a two foot oven, right? Get yourself a BIG box of aluminum foil and begin crumpling great gobs of it—not squeezing, but crumpling—so that you develop maybe an 18″ long, slightly curved shape, maybe 3½″ wide at the mouth going down to almost nothing at the tiny curlicued tip. Make a final wrap around the shape keeping the foil as smooth as possible—squeezing will cause pockets which will attract the dough and spoil everything! (If this all seems hard, remember that you can pull out your sculpture after baking and use it almost ever after, 5 or 6 times, anyway). Now let's shape a piece of parchment—about the size of half a sheet-cake pan—around the horned foil, using a stapler—you heard right—to secure where necessary (say at the base and a couple of times along the side). Have about 2″ of parchment protruding beyond the mouth of the foil.

Now let's flour our surface and roll out the dough (maybe a ¼″ thick and 2 or 3 feet long). Cut strips lengthwise (preferably with a scalloped wheel so that a design is formed when you wrap) of between 1″ to 1½″ wide. Now begin wrapping your strips around the horn. Build it from the tip up to the mouth and maybe keep the seams underneath as much as possible so

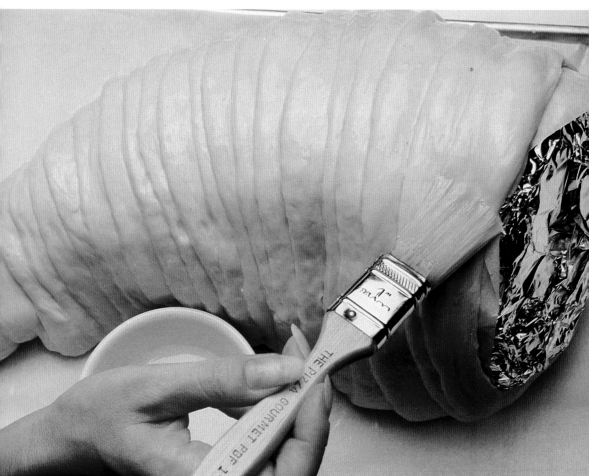

that they don't show as much. Don't be afraid to go back and fill in a loose spot. It might look a little crude after you've tucked things in, but the dough will rise when baking and so it'll smooth out. Now mix one egg with a ¼ teaspoon of salt and brush over the unbaked, as yet, horn. Oven should be at 350-375°F. Pop it in for 40-45 minutes until golden brown. Turn it occasionally (with your gloves) for an even browning. Remove the horn from the oven and let cool awhile. Turn off the oven and remove the form from the real pastry horn. Now put horn into the turned off oven for a while so that the inside loses its dampness. If you want, you can shellac/varnish your horn of plenty but it will look fine and even be edible as is!

Well, moving right along, how about filling our horn with fruits of plenty. Heat ¾ cup of frozen raspberries or strawberries (Carl prefers the deeper color of raspberries), drain off a little of their liquid and keep over heat. Then take about 16 oz. of that delightful creamy mascarpone (a little like Devonshire clotted cream—if you can't find mascarpone at your local Italian store, you might try combining cream cheese, whipping cream and ricotta). Add a teaspoon of honey and dash of vanilla (try cutting a little cross atop the cream so that honey and vanilla bleed into a nice design).

Now take some large collard and mustard green leaves and spread them stalk-end underneath the horn's mouth and leaves splayed out—maybe five large leaves total. Stuff the horn's mouth with Italian parsley and place three colors of grapes (red, purple, green) on leaves of greens. Maybe place a couple irises at the edge of the horn's mouth. This is all much nicer than your old-fashioned soggy cantaloupe or watermelon balls.

Now some big time: slice a whole pineapple—stalks and all—lengthwise in four. Take out the core from the center of each quarter. Now cut all the way around each section between meat and skin. So that the meat is detachable, but in one lump per quarter. Now vertically slice each quarter into maybe ⅜" slices. Zig-zag the slices so that they stick out maybe a ¼" side to side. Put the quarters on a large oval plate, two on one half, two on the other and stalks out. Maybe surround the pineapple sections with red-tipped lettuce, stems under the pineapple, red tips out.

Now spoon the raspberry or strawberry sauce down the middle of each pineapple quarter and maybe place another iris in the center.

A final action: On another large oval platter, place 3 different kinds of lettuce leaves so that we have three sections on the plate. On one section smother the lettuce with fresh strawberries and sliced kiwis. In the middle section place sliced apples and maybe sliced peaches. On the third section goes your dish of mascarpone dip. A couple of yellow tulips and another iris or reasonable facsimile next to the cream and you have a partially edible large art work. Maybe an exotic sherbet or Italian ice cream and BELLADOLCE... BELLADOLCE. ■

CHAPTER TWELVE

Well, now, we have our mature dough, right—four or five hours old, and the oven's been going with that magic stone in there, right, and you've got those gloves, right? Don Carlos cares that your fingers not be burned.

Now, like we said, cook it all separately, or put it all together for a party. Here's Chef Carl's cooking itinerary: starts by rolling out the focaccia dough, builds it, pops it in the oven; then creates pasta dough and makes pasta noodles after pulling out focaccia (when it's golden brown); starts Alfredo sauce; begins making calzone stuffing, then rolling out dough, makes calzone and pops in oven; starts boiling the Alfredo, then mixes sauce and noodles; pulls out calzone putting them along side focaccia, then gets set for the white pizza supreme—simple enough? ■

FOCACCIA WITH BUTTERED GARLIC & FRIENDS	
16	garlic cloves
2	tsp. melted butter
1	lb. pizza dough
	Salt and pepper
	Lightly-roasted slices of green and red pepper
	Sun-dried tomatoes packed in olive oil
	Olive oil, for brushing
	Romano cheese to sprinkle

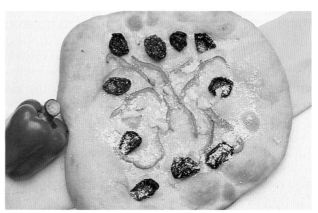

OK, we start with the focaccia, kind of a flat bread, maybe the earliest type pizza which the Romans got a hold of from the East. You can see this focaccia on the walls of early Roman buildings. Matter of fact, it was the earliest pizza to hit the U.S. of A. It's a good way to make use of leftover dough, very simple. Chef Carl had planned on only using roasted garlic with a sprinkle of Romano, but he got a little carried away by the occasion and added peppers and tomato. It's a good appetizer for the Fettucine Alfredo, but it'll stand on its own as a snack.

So here we go: Let's toss the garlic in melted butter, season with salt and pepper to taste, then pop it in a 500°F. preheated oven for maybe 25 minutes or until brown (keep the stone in the oven in preparation for the pizza).

Now for the dough: Begin by rolling out lightly on a floured surface with a large rolling pin (some purists will tell you never to use a pin 'cause you'll bruise the dough, but, ah, Carl would not be without a few spins of his big one to begin working out the dough). Because he uses high gluten flour, the chef can stretch, stretch out that stuff, working it out and out with his fists (don't feel that you have to toss it up in the sky, Dino, Carl will tell you that throwing it is just being showy). Okay, let's make it square. Put it on top of a cornmealed peel if you want and right on the stone. But Carl suggests that, for a thin pizza like this, you try a pizza screen, sort of like training wheels, a good way to get it in the oven. As the garlic cloves have cooled, remove their skins and slice or halve, if large, and

sprinkle onto dough. Add also some green and red peppers (good for Vitamin C to go along with all the other rich vitamins that you'll get from pizza). Pattern the strips out among the inner quarter sections of the square (like a symmetrical flag, architecto). Then slice pieces from the sun-dried tomatoes and add them into your pattern—unless you're into action art. Then pop that screen right in onto the preheated stone and in, hey, five or six minutes you'll take out a beautiful glistening (after you brush all edges with olive oil) golden brown puffed bread with deep brown garlic, deep green peppers and deep red peppers and tomato—a little Romano sprinkled on it as it sits on the cooling rack and fight off the grabbing hands, paesano! ∎

FETTUCINE ALFREDO

¼ lb. butter
½ tsp. white pepper
½ tsp. grated nutmeg
⅓ cup parsley leaves
1 pint heavy cream
½ Tb. salt for boiling noodles
18 oz. noodles, preferably homemade (see Introduction—pasta dough)
6 Tb. grated Romano cheese

OK. Let's go Alfredo—could be an appetizer itself, could be an appetizee avec the Focaccia. Take a large pot, put 4 or 5 quarts of water in it and bring to boil. As soon as you begin to heat the water, put a heat resistant bowl over the pot of water and place the butter in the bowl—not the water—so that it will melt as water boils underneath. As butter melts, add pepper and nutmeg, all but a few sprigs of the parsley leaves and stir in the heavy cream.

Now, when the sauce becomes warm, remove the bowl and salt the water. Carl says no olive oil—it'll coat the pasta so that the sauce won't stick to it—so just use a little salt. Put the noodles into the boiling water. If they're homemade they'll only need to be in there maybe 30 seconds—don't want it to get all mushy (store-purchased noodles will take longer, see directions on package!). Drain the noodles in a colander—in the sink of course, then place it in the warm bowl of sauce and mix with forks. Sprinkle some grated Romano onto individual dishes or onto mixture in bowl. This is a hard sheep's milk cheese, a little, you know, sharper, tangier than your Parmesan, but not too bitter. Get it in solid form and grate it yourself if you want da capo line. A few more parsley leaves on top and fight off your dinner guests—no wonder, that Mr. Thomas Jefferson was a pasta freak. But don't stop, you need to work on the calzone. ∎

5 CHEESE CALZONE DELIGHT

1 lb. basic pizza dough
1 28-oz. can Italian-style plum tomatoes
Salt for dehydrating tomatoes
3 oz. sliced fresh mushrooms
1 tsp. fresh basil
1 tsp. marjoram
2 tsp. oregano
Parsley leaves
1 cup whole milk ricotta cheese
3 oz. freshly grated mozarella cheese
3 oz. bel paese cheese
1 oz. gorgonzola cheese
¼ cup freshly grated Romano cheese
4 oz. broccoli tops
Additional grated Romano cheese, for sprinkling

AH, YES, Tony, let's try the calzone. Well—let's get our clean hands messy. Remember, we prepared our dough a few hours ago, giving it that friendly little kick like a used car salesman from, uh, Detroit. So we'll start on the stuffing. The canned Italian-style tomatoes must be drained in a colander for ½ an hour after being sprinkled with a little weep inducing salt. Squeeze them until completely dry and roll them tight in a kitchen towel to get all the moisture out (or, you could use sun-dried tomatoes). And don't soak the mushrooms to clean them, just use a damp cloth or a brush—don't want a soggy stuffing! Combine mushrooms and tomatoes with spices and parsley; then ricotta and cubed mozzarella plus cubed bel paese (that means "beautiful country" and it's a beautiful creamy cheese, Carl wants you to know) and gorgonzola, like bel paese a northern Italian cow-milk cheese. Then the grated Romano and the broccoli flowers—well, pick your order. Now, smoosh, bambino, smoosh. That's right, get messy with those hands and knead it all together so that you end up with a cheese-ball effect, nice and DRY, remember.

OK, now for the dough. Take out that big pin and roll it out maybe ¼- or ⅜-inch thick—your choice, on floured surface. Don't be afraid of that flour.

You can poke holes in a jar top and shake the flour out like that— a cute homespun touch Carl likes to think.

Cut dough with a four-inch cookie cutter and let's stuff 'em; in fact, let's OVERSTUFF them. Too little and that middle is gonna melt away too, you know, "where's the stuffing?" So that big ball of stuffing is in the middle of the dough and we'll press down the middle of said stuffing with thumbs and bring the edge of the dough out and over with the fingers so that you can join the dough edges together into a ball—well, let's say into a kind of oyster shell with the mouth pressed down into corrugated pinches. That's the first seal. For seal #2 use a, get this, a ¾- or 1-inch wallpaper seam roller (that's "seam-roller," not "steam-roller"). And, remembering to use enough flour to prevent sticking, roll down the edge again. Third seal of the mouth is what Carl calls his pinch and roll. He pinches the mouth flat and then folds it back into braids toward the body so that you might imagine that mouth now to be the wreathed head of some Roman maiden. But enough of the poetry. Place the calzones on a parchment-covered cookie sheet (UNOILED). Make a slit of about an inch and a half on top of the dough and place the cookie sheet right on top of the stone. Bake from 10-15 minutes until golden brown—remember those gloves—put them on the cooling rack and sprinkle a little Romano (or Parmesan if you really want) and there you are, padrone. ■

ALL WHITE CHEESY PIZZA WITH CHICKEN AND WALNUTS

2	chicken breasts
2	oz. olive oil with garlic
¼	tsp. white pepper
3	oz. onion, sliced
¾	cup mozzarella cheese, cubed
19	oz. pizza dough
	Olive oil for brushing
3	oz. red peppers
3	oz. mushrooms, sliced
1	small eggplant, finely sliced
½	cup zucchini, thin-sliced
2	oz. walnuts
⅓	cup bel paese cheese
3	oz. Romano cheese or Parmesan cheese, grated

OK—this is your great white MOBY PIZZA. Let's attack the chicken. To debone them, Carlo separates meat from bones with his thumbs, nothing fancy, then rips them away. Better yet, says the Prince of Machiavelli, buy your chicken deboned! Pull off skin and cut meat into, say, one by two inch sections—should have about four ounces. Sauté chicken in skillet with garlic and oil, seasoning with pepper, until pink has disappeared. Also sauté the onions.

Carl likes his mozzarella—the real McCoy is from water buffalo milk, they being brought to Rome from the East during Roman Empire-time. And forget that imitation, artificial-colored, preservative-filled stuff that's foisted off as mozzarella—this is the Pizza Gourmet you're following. So Chef Carl likes to have his mozzarella diced rather than sliced, easier to spread around that way. He just cubes it and drops it into the food processor and turns on the dice blade.

Now roll out, stretch out the dough (same as with focaccia) but a little thicker if you want, and put it on the cornmealed peel. If it won't slide around, just bless the peel with cornmeal where it sticks. Brush dough with olive oil to create a barrier. Now let's lay down our base of

96

mozzarella, then scatter the browned chicken, sautéed onions, peppers and mushrooms. Add eggplant slices and brush each with garlic in oil. Put zucchini slices near outside of pizza square. Scatter on walnuts (if they're too strong for your taste, try almonds, or whatever). Maybe if you're really creating a monster, drop on the bel paese. Make sure, again, that the dough will slide and put the peel in the oven at a 25° angle downward and, touching the stone at the back of the oven, jerk the peel away. Bake 10-12 minutes at that preheated 500° and you'll have a bella, bella golden-brown pizza. Take it from the stone with the peel, place it on a cooling rack, sprinkle with Romano or Parmesan (that's from Parma, Italy, right), brush the edges with a little olive oil for softening, and that's amore. Finally, slice up the pizza in squares, maybe 3″ or 4″ by pushing the cutting wheel away from you—and dinner is served. ■

CHAPTER THIRTEEN

LAGNIAPPE

Well, have you gone all the way straight through or cut back and forth and become your very own pizza gourmet (non sa fingere non sa regnare)? Maybe you've even had a party and combined different items from different chapters? Well, would Carl—who is so considerate when he caters a party as to make the pizzas square so that the toppings won't slurp down into the curlicues of fancy shoe designs and to keep reminding you to bless the pizza, Guido—leave without just a coupla pastabilities for your next bash? So here's the envoi: How about a Calzone that's fried rather than baked on the stone? ■

FRIED CALZONE

1½	cups ricotta cheese
2	egg yolks
¼	cup Romano cheese, grated
¾	cup ham, diced
6	whole Italian tomatoes, squeezed dry
1	clove garlic, minced
10	leaves Italian parsley, chopped
	Salt & pepper to taste
1	lb. pizza dough
1	qt. vegetable oil

COMBINE all ingredients but the dough and oil in a bowl and smoosh together. Roll out the dough and cut out and fill the calzones following normal filling and sealing methods (see Chapter 12). Heat the oil in a large skillet (you can check the temp by dipping in the tip of a wooden spoon—if you see bubbles it's ready for the calzones to be gently dropped in and fritter away until they're a golden brown). Don't feed them to Rover until they cool off a little. ■

CRABMEAT & SPAGHETTI

Can you make the pasta as per the Introduction, run it through to #5 in the machine then make noodles? Then:

	Leaves from 1 bunch parsley, chopped
3	cloves garlic, chopped
6	tsp. butter
	Salt & pepper to taste
1	lb. crabmeat, picked

MELT the butter in a pan and add the garlic. Add the parsley and sauté for 3 minutes, adding salt and pepper. Then transfer the mixture to a bowl.

Bring the crab and water to a boil and remove. Save the water in which to now cook the noodles. You'll need an insert, because we'd like you to remove the noodles and add them to the butter/parsley/garlic mixture. Then reheat the crabmeat in the water for 2 more minutes before tossing with noodles, etc. in the bowl.

Here are a couple of dips, Benito, that could go with fruits and, of course, pizza and champagne. ■

FOR RED AND GREEN GRAPES

MINT WITH RICOTTA:

½	cup ricotta cheese
¼	cup confectioners' sugar
1	Tb. fresh mint, chopped

That one you should smoosh, the next, for red or black raspberries, you should stir together:

ROSE CREAM:

1	tsp. rose water
1	Tb. confectioners' sugar
½	cup sour cream

SO don't stop making your swampy dough preps, your peppers of delight, your horns of plenty. Nor stop dreaming, along with Il Carlo, that Habeba from Chapter and Show 9 glides toward your own private counter across a cornmealed floor. ■

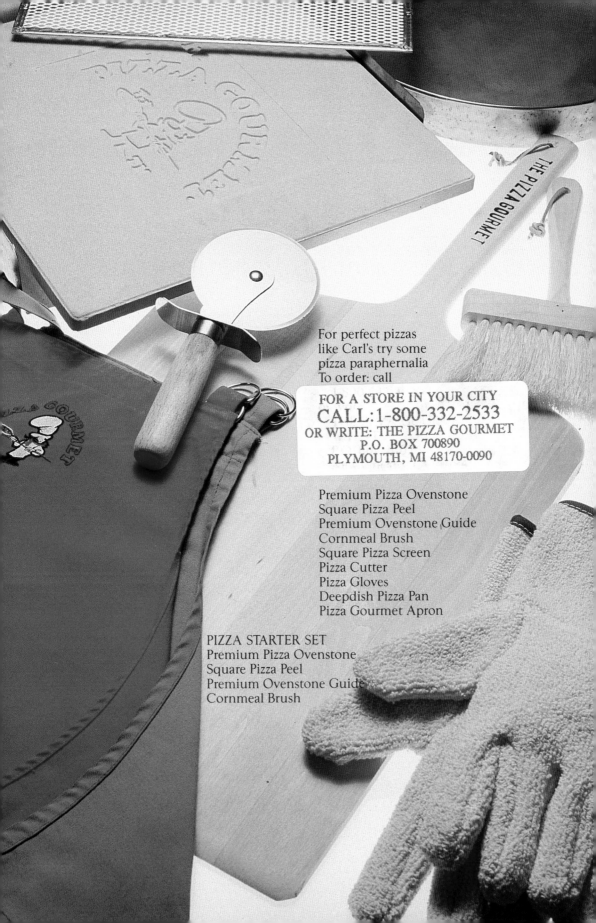

For perfect pizzas
like Carl's try some
pizza paraphernalia
To order: call

Premium Pizza Ovenstone
Square Pizza Peel
Premium Ovenstone Guide
Cornmeal Brush
Square Pizza Screen
Pizza Cutter
Pizza Gloves
Deepdish Pizza Pan
Pizza Gourmet Apron

PIZZA STARTER SET
Premium Pizza Ovenstone
Square Pizza Peel
Premium Ovenstone Guide
Cornmeal Brush

THE PIZZA GOURMET

Author: Robert Arlett
Chef: Carl Oshinsky

Designer/Art Director: Bob Coleman
Stylist: Kathy Coleman
Head Photographer: Kathy Coleman
Photographers: Barry Muniz, Cliff Roland
Typographer: Forstall Typographers

Adapted from the PBS Television Series
THE PIZZA GOURMET
WYES-TV   New Orleans

Producers: Lyn Adams, Paul Combel
Executive Producer: Mike LaBonia